It's Just A Damn Date!!!

Why We Expect Too Much Too Soon

Per Mickey —
Be inspired + laugh endlessly!

Copyright © 2006 Tariiq Omari Walton for
Omari Books
www.omaribooks.com
Second Edition: 2010

A Division of Infinite Possibilities Entertainment, LLC

Infinite Possibilities Entertainment, LLC

International Standard Book Number: 0-9762101-1-8

Note: This book contains the opinions and ideas of the author. It is intended to provide helpful and informative material on the subject matter covered. It is sold with the understanding that the author and publisher are not engaged in rendering professional services in the book. If the reader requires personal assistance or advice, a competent professional should be consulted.

Printed in the U.S.A.

This is dedicated to
My little sister
Elena,
My nephews
Malik, Mekai, & Jay,
And my niece
Anaiya.
Always stay one step ahead of the rest!

Acknowledgments

There is a whole world of people I need to acknowledge, but no one more than my family and friends for all of their endless support. Since publishing **Broken,** you guys have been there for me in everyway possible, and let me know that I am far from being alone on this literary voyage.

A big, big, BIG thank you goes out to my editors Erica Kennedy and Dr. Constance Elena Cannon, better known as Momma Red (the woman who gave me birth and would not allow *me* to *give birth* to anything second rate again). The two of you made this book shine!

A special "Hey, Hey, Hey, Hey" shout out goes to one of the bestestestest friends a guy like me could ever have, Miss Thema A. Wilson, for all of her patience in helping me design the book cover. I know it was a long and arduous journey, but we pulled off something magnificent, don't you think?

Thank you to my mentor Lynn Johnson for all of your positive energy, understanding, and encouragement. You are truly a beautiful and inspirational soul, and one of the world's rarest jewels.

To all of my readers, thank you for not losing respect for me after getting the first dose of what was in my twisted mind!

Big ups to my homie, Nicole Lobban: thank you, thank you, thank you for the hours upon hours of helping me build up and tear down what relationships are and are not. I don't know where you gained all of your peculiar knowledge, but I thank those guys too.

And I would be the biggest fraud on the planet if I didn't give a shout out to my inspiration and muse: EVERYONE!! Thanks to all of my friends and family who have endured endless bad relationships to provide me with ample material in writing **It's Just A Damn Date**. A great deal of appreciation goes out to all of the wonderful strangers I've come across who opened up their battle wounds and let their stories pour onto my lap. Thank you to the many people whom I surveyed and interviewed and who took part in my focus groups. Your information, wisdom, and insight have been invaluable. And a special thank you has to be mentioned to all of the women and for all of the fantastic, terrible, fair, and indifferent dates I have ever been on. You've opened my eyes to so many things, particularly the understanding that **IT WAS JUST A DAMN DATE**!

Table of Contents

Preface

Dating. Courtship. Romancing. The pursuit of relationship building. How would I describe the average American's approach to this seemingly simple, yet timeless, act? One word says it best: DYSFUNCTIONAL!

Face it. You have absolutely no idea what you are doing. You can't seem to get it right no matter how hard or how many times you try. You can't figure it out and—even worst—you simply don't know why. It seems like you are caught in this cycle of meeting people, "loving people," losing people, then lying in bed for an extra hour every morning trying desperately to make some sense out of what happened because you've become (once again) an emotional wreck.

A few weeks later, you've found enough stamina to throw yourself back into the social scene, where you "luckily" meet someone new, love again, lose again, and—you guessed it— find yourself back in bed for an extra hour each morning wondering what went wrong. Accept it. You, too, have become yet another victim of dating's "vicious cycle."

The bottom line is that we are amid a cultural epidemic of bad relationships. More than fifty percent (50%) of all American marriages end in divorce. And if your first marriage doesn't work, the chances of maintaining a successful second or third marriage are even slimmer.

Now, if you are still not convinced this is indeed a serious epidemic, let me put it in simpler terms: If you were given a 2 in 5 chance to live, your hopes of survival wouldn't leave you feeling too optimistic now would it? Exactly! The same goes for the staggering statistics on marriage and divorce. Yet marriage is supposed to be the zenith of our relationship journey? If so, we've got a lot of work to do.

Any successful relationship begins with YOU. But guess what? Any bad relationship begins with YOU as well. Recognize that the seeds you plant in infertile grounds will yield bad crops. And those you sow in fertile grounds will bring forth great product.

Therefore, my mission is to till the grounds; bring the healthy soil to the surface, so those crops can have a fighting chance at a successful harvest. Yes, these growing crops will still have to endure droughts, floods, tornados, hurricanes, early frosts, and locusts before their harvesting, but their roots will be strong and their base will be sturdy.

Just think of me as Farmer Riiqo, because the soil in this case is your mind and **It's Just A Damn Date** is the tiller.

****

A point needs to be made first, however, about the correlation between the advances in our society and the root causes of the failure of sustainable relationships. Due to the technological advances of the second half of the 20th century, we now live in a society of ease, choice, and opportunity. Today people regularly change their careers whereas a few decades ago, it was not unusual to stay at the same job or in the same position until retirement or death. But with more lucrative employment opportunities and higher pay scales (read: bigger paychecks), we purchase fancier cars, buy bigger homes, and relocate to new areas more readily than our grandparents ever did, who have owned the same car and house and lived in the same neighborhood their entire lives.

With the societal advances of the past half-century, everything has become disposable and/or replaceable. We live in a consumer-based economy and to practice anything different would be counter-cultural; to believe anything else would be counter-intuitive. Because of these same freedoms and advancements, the need for marriage and relationships has changed as well. Where marriage was once a necessity for security, status, and opportunity, it is no longer a need but a desire. And just as swiftly as our desire for material possessions change, so does our desire for commitment.

The concept of staying married until death has always been a part of our society's tradition and culture. But like most traditions in our society that have been turned upside down since the Great Depression and the Second World War, the ideology of staying with one mate "until death do you part" has suffered as well.

****

Another point has to be made about the correlation between the rise of safe and reliable birth control and the decline of committed relationships. The introduction of the birth control pill in the 1950's (at the peak of the Baby Boom) lead to the sexual revolution of the 60's and 70's, where people were able to explore their sexuality without the concerns of unwanted pregnancies. For the first time in history, the general population could engage in intercourse and not worry about any of its consequences.

In a world lacking the Pill, this was very risqué behavior; not because of the stigma attached to being sexually promiscuous, but because of the series of events that were likely to follow such as unwanted pregnancies and forced unions. This is not to say that folks from earlier times didn't take the chance (discussed in the chapter "Marriage is Overrated: Your Grandmother is Just Waiting for your Grandfather to Die!" in Book Three of the Love Hostage Series) It is just without such fears, people could boldly participate in sexual activities without having to establish a commitment of any kind.

****

In writing this book, I want to be very upfront and honest with you. What I am proposing will be pretty confrontational, not only because it goes against the instincts of human nature, but because it can easily conflict with human biology. What I am suggesting with **It's Just A Damn Date** is our need to adjust our thinking so that it doesn't continue to run counter to our societal and technological advances. In many ways, nature has its own agenda that science often tries to ignore. Ironically, the only thing helping to bridge that gap between the nature of things and our cultural advances *is* science!

The way our culture is developing around the themes of education, professional advancement, and financial independence, many women are choosing to bare children later in life. Unfortunately, biology has not changed and, often times, waiting to do so can prove risky if not impossible. Therefore, this sociological/biological conflict continuously plays a major role in the complications of dating and marriage—a conflict we must earnestly find a solution to if the theory of man and woman uniting (and staying together until death indeed parts them) is to continue to exist.

****

The path that I offer isn't an easy one. As a matter of fact, it is hard as hell because it takes a great deal of discipline and self-reflection—something we often neglect to develop within ourselves or properly instill in our children. My hope is that we all learn to be more honest with ourselves and our mates, and recognize the truth behind the situations in which we find ourselves. Ultimately, **It's Just A Damn Date's** main objectives are to help each of us be more realistic about the potential outcomes of our dates, and introduce a healthier way for men and women to interact while on their quest to "happily ever after."

Introduction

One of the most complicated things about growing up is figuring out how to deal with other people. It is a process that begins as soon as we exit the womb, and it continues throughout over lives. In fact, our interactions become much more complex the older we get, and dating definitely does nothing to alleviate these difficulties.

When navigating through the rocky waves of dating and courtship, it is important to have a sound understanding of the common terminology we use when doing so. Therefore, I've selected the following 13 terms for three reasons: 1) I like odd numbers; 2) everyone is afraid of the number 13; and 3) I hate lists that end with 10 items. Like comedian/philosopher George Carlin once said, that's great for marketing but it isn't always accurate or honest. More importantly, I've chosen these 13 terms because they seem to be the most significantly ambiguous and disputable words used when dating and courting. Webster's Dictionary defines these terms as such:

- Date - a meeting arranged in advance; to make or have a social engagement with someone of the opposite sex;

- Courting - to attempt to gain the favor of by flattery or attention; to attempt to gain the affections or love of: woo;

- Single - one who is unmarried; of or pertaining to celibacy; unaccompanied by another or others;

- Love - an intense affectionate concern for another person; an intense sexual desire for another person;

- Like - to find pleasant; enjoy; to feel an attraction, tenderness, or affection for; be fond of;

- Infatuation - having an irrational passion or attraction; to cause to behave foolishly;

- Expectation - to look forward to the probable occurrence or appearance of; to consider likely or certain; to consider obligatory: require;

- Intention - an aim that guides action; a plan of action;

- Agenda - a list of things to be done;

- Disappoint - to fail to satisfy the hope, desire, or expectation of;

- Fool - one deficient in judgment, sense, or understanding; one who acts unwise; a feeble-minded person;

- Game - a scheme, a plan; a form of play, amusement;

- Player - one who plays a specific game; an actor.

Now that we know what Webster's has to say, let's discuss how many of us really understand and apply these terms accurately.

"Dating" is simply the act of going out and enjoying someone's company without the expectations of a relationship developing or more happening subsequent to that night or that moment. A date doesn't establish a commitment of any kind. The only expectations you should have of a date are undivided attention, civility, honesty, and an enjoyable time. (*Rules for dating will be discussed later in the book.*)

"Courting" or courtship is the act of pursuing a deeper, more meaningful relationship with someone you have been dating. For reasons that will also be discussed later, courtship is a one-way street, and for a relationship to be successful, it must be the man who courts the woman.

The word "single" is probably the most disputable of all dating terms. Using only Webster's definition of this word leaves the term open to vast interpretations that can make it difficult to determine one's real status. A person may consider himself or herself single (never married), but dating or courting one individual exclusively. Whereas a once married person who's separated or divorced may also consider himself or herself single as well. These types of interchangeable definitions prove there's a lot you need to know about your suitor before you begin designing your wedding invitations.

"Love" is also a term whose meaning is hard to characterize with one all-encompassing definition. But love is much more than just a word; it is probably one of the strongest emotions anyone can ever experience. It is an entity so strong, it directly or indirectly effects every other emotion we have.

The emotion often associated with the feeling of love can many times be confused with "liking" and "infatuation." These two terms are often very well hidden by an individual's intentions, and can remain so well into marriage. The differences can simply be a matter of degrees, but the factors that establish the truest forms of love are much greater than just what you feel. To determine what it is that you are feeling, you really need to understand why you feel the way you do. For example, when you say you are in love with someone, is it because of the way that person makes you feel or is it because you are truly concerned with that person's well being, oft times more than your own?

Regardless, the one thing that can put an irreparable crack in the foundation of any relationship is a misplaced "expectation". The expectations one has going into a date are often made complicated by their desires to have their entire lives fulfilled in an instant. Even our simplest desires like lust and hunger can create unrealistic expectations and lead to disappointing dates. For example, if you are invited to a movie, don't expect to be fed too. Applying the definition above, your date isn't obliged to feed you as well as pay for your movie ticket. Your "intentions" and having an "agenda" for those intentions fall along the same line as expectations. To start a date already knowing what you want to get out of it doesn't allow it to be what it is meant to be.

What you often find as a result of seeking these unknown gains and underserved rewards as stated above is someone who's made himself or herself a *disanointed* "fool." You can become someone's fool, you can make someone your fool, or you can make a fool of yourself. This is because you either don't practice good judgment, don't understand the circumstances, or ignore the truth of a situation for any number of feeble-minded reasons in an effort to get what you want. Sadly, the thing about being a fool is that everyone else sees it way before you do.

On a date, when someone has these *expectations*, *intentions*, and *agendas*, but not a hint of honesty to go with them, what you have is known as "game." Unfortunately, that is what dating has become: one big game filled with a myriad of "players." Players are indeed actors that behave this way; people who act like they are something they are not, to fulfill their intentions and expectations without giving much thought to the consequences that can occur from doing so. Sadly, this is the world in which dating and courtship now exist.

So to become better daters and suitors, not only must we understand the meaning behind the terms that describe our actions, but we need to apply them to our experiences so that we can begin to see ourselves, acknowledge our mistakes, and discover ways to change our behavior for the better. It is going to be a lot of work, but if you are up for the challenge, the rewards will be well worth it.

Are you ready? If so, let's begin....

Reggie & Phoebe

Sitting with her feet on Reggie's lap, Phoebe pointed to her favorite football player from the Express coming back onto the field, and Reggie boos in kind. The televised football game had been brutal and she feared that Michael "Rhythm" Jones might have been lost for the season. Such a disaster would have thrown her statistics for her fantasy football league team completely in the toilet.

Phoebe bought her 60-inch plasma television for laid back times like this. Every Sunday that season, she'd kept company with Reggie, a twin spirit in the world of sports fanaticism. Their new doubleheader tradition often led to mounds of popcorn littering the carpet around the couch as they playful wrestled for command over the remote control.

On each morning (not just Sundays), when she woke with the alluring, comedic man in her bed, Phoebe made sure she was up before him to guarantee she looked her best when he finally opened his eyes. With her make-up perfect, her night scarf removed, and her hair coiffed, she would often bring Reggie breakfast in bed.

Even though Reggie thoroughly enjoyed spending time with Phoebe because of their mutual interests and her culinary expertise, it was her skills beneath the sheets that further set her apart from every woman in his past. Watching her drink from a glass of apple juice, Reggie admitted to himself that he had never met someone that was so willing to please when the expectations were usually vice versa. Phoebe was beautiful, talented, intelligent, humorous, and made three times as much money as he; she could have easily bought herself the royal treatment she bestowed upon others, but she chose to bestow it on him.

****

Two weeks prior, Phoebe had invited Reggie to her parent's home for a dinner she was preparing for her mother's birthday. He was really impressed with the closeness of her family and the way Phoebe interacted with her niece and two nephews. Picturing a beautiful future with the athletic, energetic, overachiever didn't take much imagination.

While the entire family sat around the television after the wonderful meal, Phoebe snuck Reggie off to the laundry room for a quickie. The way she went after him, you would have thought they hadn't had sex four times before they arrived at her parent's house. It was this kind of risqué behavior that kept Reggie coming back.

****

During the middle of Reggie's regular Saturday afternoon basketball game with his friends, Jabari picked up the ball and stopped play for a moment. Everyone turned to see what had caught his attention so strongly that it would make him blow a fast-break chance at a lay up. To Reggie's surprise it was Phoebe. She waved at him and he waved back, even though he knew he was going to hear about it from the fellas later.

After play resumed, Reggie was taken down by a hard foul, and Phoebe popped out of her seat and ran to his side. His friends helped him to stand, but seeing that he couldn't put any weight on his right foot, Phoebe told the fellas to take Reggie to her truck.

Sitting in the emergency room for seven hours, Phoebe stayed by Reggie's side throughout the entire process. By the time they finally saw a doctor, Reggie's ankle had ballooned to the size of a softball. X-rays revealed that nothing was broken, and Phoebe joked that he needed to suck up the pain like Reggie demanded "Rhythm" Jones to do during the previous week's game.

Phoebe drove Reggie back to her home and sat him down on the couch where she elevated his bad leg on a stack of pillows. Wearing an air caste, Reggie was happy to let Phoebe do what she did best: take care of the people to whom she gave her heart. While he flipped through the channels on the TV, Phoebe returned from the kitchen with a bowl filled with a warm walnut brownie and Reggie's favorite Rum Raisin ice cream.

As they sat quietly together on the couch, watching a rerun of *I Spy*, Reggie rested his head on Phoebe's lap while she stroked his head. Phoebe had never felt closer to Reggie than she did at that very moment, and asked him if he'd like to stay with her until his ankle felt better.

Phoebe watched Reggie's face as he remained silent to process her question. As he prepared to answer, he carefully took his elevated foot off of the pillows and sat up on the couch. Graciously, Reggie thanked her but revealed that he had made a date for Monday night, and her suggestion was not conducive to his plans.

The Interesting Chick

There are many factors that stimulate the move from the dating phase of a budding relationship into courtship; some elements can be very significant, while others may seem pretty shallow. Nonetheless, when determining whether or not we are interested in pursing a more meaningful relationship with someone, these factors are the key to our decision.

These influential factors vary and carry a different weight according to the individual making the decision. Many of us create mental checklists of characteristics a potential suitor or mate should possess in order to make that next step. On that list are items that we are willing to be flexible about, and items we refuse to compromise on.

This is the true essence of dating. It is through our experiences and varying interactions with different people that we are able to develop these lists. Over time and through multiple interactions, we begin to conclude what factors are the most vital, and we begin to have a healthier understanding of what kind of person best suits us.

Commonalities
The most significant factors we all look for are things that we share in common with the other person. It is important to be with someone who shares some, if not most, of our same interests because regardless of what else is happening we will always have those things that we can enjoy together (and relationships are about togetherness). We are not necessarily looking for our clone, but we want a balance where we can share new experiences together as well as find joy in our commonalities.

In that same vein, we have to be able to distinguish the difference between those who appear to share some of our interests but are in fact only doing so to appease us. This kind of "dishonesty" allows suitors to get closer, and even though their intentions may be pure, it serves no one when people aren't being themselves (see the chapter: **Hiding Self**).

My New Me
Not only do we develop a checklist of things we want in a potential mate through our dating experiences, we also create a checklist for ourselves based on these same interactions. We learn a great deal about ourselves this way. We observe how people respond to us and why; we discern what interest's people have, particularly the "types" that we tend to be attracted to and the types that are attracted to us; and we discover some things about ourselves that we might need to change if we wish to have a successful relationship one day.

All of these checklists allow us to be reflective. As human beings, we are meant to be flexible enough in our approach to

4

life that we are able to make changes and adjustments where necessary. This contributes greatly to our growth and development as potential husbands or wives, as well as better more complete people overall. Anyone too rigid and nonconforming is not experiencing life; even a mountain changes its face.

Where we need to be careful is when we begin to change for other people. There's a big difference between making a change because we realize we need to be more open minded to new experiences, and making a change just to please someone else. Compromise in any relationship is natural but changing your interests, desires, dreams and the basic core of who you are to appease someone else is not. Remember you will never find true satisfaction with yourself or the other person if the change is forced.

Insecurities

Many of us feel the need to change who we are to gain attention or respect from others because of our many insecurities. We live in a hypercritical society where it is easy to question things about ourselves and underestimate our self-worth. This translates into additional complications when dealing with other people, particularly in dating circumstances.

Both men and women suffer great insecurities. There are things we don't like about ourselves, things we don't understand about ourselves, and things we feel others may not (or sincerely don't) like about us, too. This is an unfortunate dilemma that is not bound by age or gender. But what is most unfortunate about it is our approach at correcting it.

Many times we will focus on the more superficial aspects of who we are when we try to face our insecurities, and these issues typically concern our appearance. Sadly, media and advertisers alike are aware of this and have used our insecurities to their advantage by producing more and more images of what we should be, in turn forcing us to spend more and more money in hopes of achieving that "look."

We try to change our appearance by buying bigger houses and more luxurious cars; we buy expensive clothing to make us look slimmer; we become members at gyms to burn off extra weight and build sexier-looking bodies; and we pay for expensive plastic surgery to cut off, tuck, pull, or suck out those things that we can't change any other way. But none of these extremisms are necessary. As young, single, professionals, why buy a five-bedroom house when we are the only ones in it? Or purchase SUVs and luxury sedans with no one else to tote around but ourselves? One word: image.

We definitely need to do all we can to build and support our nation's infrastructure, but at what expense to our sanity? We can buy all of the make-up, cars, and jewelry in the world, but we have done nothing to correct our insecurities inside. All we've done is cover them up.

If we intend on truly relieving ourselves of our insecurities, it is important to figure out why we feel insecure in the first place. We must examine what those insecurities are, where they came from, and plot a way to make the appropriate changes. This means looking in the mirror and facing up to the truths about who we are and what we've done. That takes much more courage than spending money on a house we can't afford.

Becoming

In our story, we aren't told much about Phoebe's life, and we don't know what, if any, insecurities might have been plaguing her. What we do see is that she has many of the qualities an average man may find appealing: she is caring; she is sexual; she can cook; she has a great relationship with her family; and she loves sports.

Many women often have major disagreements with men over their obsessive love of sports, but this hardly seemed the case with Phoebe. She seemed genuinely enthusiastic over them.

There's a common belief within women's circles that the way to a man's heart is with food, sex, and sports (not necessarily in that order), and it seemed liked Phoebe wasn't coming up short in any of these areas. But there's a twist that women who support this theory have not traditionally taken into consideration. That is, they have focused so much on feeding a man's basic physical needs that they forgot to consider his emotional needs as well.

We all put in so much time changing ourselves to be more desirable to others that when we are rejected we continue to question ourselves and our worth. The fact is there may be nothing wrong with us at all. The simple reason a relationship may not have been established after what seemed like a successful dating experience or courtship usually comes down to timing.

No matter how perfect Phoebe was, if Reggie wasn't ready for a relationship, then he just wasn't ready and there was nothing she could say, do, or change to get him there. At the same time, Reggie shouldn't be made out to be a bad person for his frame of mind and he shouldn't feel guilty, either, *unless* he was leading her on. If he was being upfront with his feelings and actions, then he was by no means in the wrong. If he wasn't, well, that's another story.

What they saw for their future might have been different. An interesting dynamic that eventually arises in these types of situations is that when someone like Reggie is ready to settle down and be in a committed relationship (and he will), he'll remember Phoebe and reel from anguish for letting such a *perfect* woman go. He'll hunt her down and try to reestablish a connection, but by then the timing might not be good on her end.

For the time being, though, each has to respect where they are in their particular "relationship lives." Think of it like being at the DMV on a Saturday. Phoebe's ticket number is about to be called, where as Reggie is still standing near the back of the ticket line that snakes out the door, around the corner, and down the block. If he happens to instantaneously become ready (like men typically do when the time is right), he'll skip the entire line and walk right up to the service window. But as things exist, he can't even see Phoebe for the "perfect" woman she is.

We make a common mistake in believing that everyone wants the same thing. But not everyone wants to have children (and everyone shouldn't; some people simply aren't meant to be parents) and not everyone wants to be in a relationship (try sitting down with a recent divorcee and ask them *their* views). But more so, even if these are parts of life people do want to explore, they may not want to experience them right now.

In the end, even though there may be things about ourselves that people don't like, we shouldn't let that affect who we are and how we live. We are not always the cause for things not working out; as mentioned earlier, it may just be a matter of timing. However, we must take hold of our genuine insecurities and discover our true value first; accepting who we are and respecting others for the decisions they choose to make regarding their own lives is paramount.

To The Point

- We use dating experiences to develop "checklists" that help determine suitable personality traits in potential mates
- Sharing common interests can give a couple more things to enjoy together when new experiences are absent
- Be careful of people who only appear to share your interests
- We learn a great deal about our own personality traits through our dating experiences
- Developing checklists helps us to be more reflective

- We should be flexible in our approach to developing relationships
- Don't force change on yourself or anyone else
- Recognize when you are making changes to better yourself versus to appease someone else
- Compromise in relationships is natural, but don't underestimate your self-worth
- Acknowledge and face your insecurities instead of covering them with expensive toys and other trinkets
- A relationship's success or failure may have nothing to do with you or your personality traits
- "Timing" can be a major contributor to the evolution of a romance from dating and courting to an actual relationship
- Clarity in one's relationship intensions are essential in that romance's evolutionary process
- Don't assume that your partner is on your same page and wants exactly what you want
- Respect other's decisions not to be in a committed relationship, and determine whether you should stay or move on

A Better Move

Take your time in giving of yourself. Build slowly.

Contemplative Corner

1. Name five (5) appealing personality traits you have discovered in others through dating
2. Name five (5) of your own personality traits you've discovered through dating or while in a relationship
3. In what ways have you changed to appease someone or has someone changed to appease you?

4. How has timing affected the success or failure of your past relationships?
5. What excuses have people used to inform you and what excuses have you used to inform others that either you or they were not ready to be in a relationship?

Terri & Brandon

The sound of shoe heels clicking on the wooden floor planks echoed in the air while Terri and Brandon sipped on two cups of Italian Ice Water. The boardwalk was packed; normal for that time of day and year, and a warm breeze captured the mellow scent of fresh cut grass from nearby Thurgood Marshall Park. The young couple took a seat on a bench overlooking the bay, being sure to leave the appropriate amount of space between them allowed for a first date.

Meeting a week ago at a mutual friend's birthday party, where Brandon kept Terri cornered with conversation for most of the night, the words flowed between the two of them like water down a tropical falls. Terri shared her dreams of finishing graduate school with a Master's degree in social work and charging into the work force to save as many children from broken homes as she possibly could—an accomplishment she hoped to achieve before she turned 30 and started planning for a family.

However, what she failed to tell Brandon was that she'd take a husband in a minute if it meant she wouldn't have to work at all. The only reason why she was even in graduate school was to increase her dating marketability. She knew men loved women who gave the appearance of being independent but still secretly longed to be taken care of.

Brandon admired Terri's strength but also recognized her vulnerability. Her sense of compassion was overwhelming, and he decided to tell her his own story of needing to drop out of college to take care of his mother when she became ill. Brandon wanted to go back to school, but his mother's medical bills ate into the family's ability to pay for his education.

Now that she was better, he was determined to get back in and finish what he started.

The only problem with Brandon's story is that it had a few gaps. In reality, Brandon got thrown out of school for selling marijuana on campus his sophomore year and all of the ensuing legal problems stressed his mother out so much that she became ill. He really had no intentions of going back, but he knew that women love a man who can remain ambitious in the face of adversity. Brandon had told his "story" so many times, he was beginning to believe it himself. However, he felt if he continued to "sell" his story, he would eventually find a woman who would "pay" for it, as well as his dream of opening up a garage for sports cars.

****

The wind shifted and began blowing over the bay, bringing with it the chill of the coming night. Terri snuggled beneath Brandon's arm, which he let fall across her shoulders like a shawl, and the warmth of his body comforted her. As Brandon caressed her arm, Terri was reminded of the last man to touch her in that way, and explained the circumstances surrounding her last break up.

As the story would have it, the man she was with for three years cheated on her, and despite her best efforts to forgive him and salvage their relationship, he continued to break her heart and finally left her for good eight months later. Only, she forgot to tell Brandon that she cheated on him first, and despite his best efforts, she couldn't stay out of other men's beds either.

****

Angling to watch the sun set in the southwest, Terri laid her back against Brandon's chest, and his arms wrapped around her torso. Feeling the intimacy growing, Brandon revealed his longing to share many more such beautiful moments with someone truly special, noting that not everyone could appreciate the romantic nature of a setting sun and sweet moments like the one they were sharing. Oddly, he had said something similar to a woman named Raquel the night before....

Brandon had just sat down after eating a sumptuous dinner Raquel had prepared for him. Finding a book of matches, he lit the candles on her coffee and end tables, and settled into a spot on her loveseat while he waited for her to finish doing the dishes. The wind was howling; slamming branches from a nearby tree against the window as a storm formed in the sky. At the first crack of thunder, Raquel bolted from the kitchen and onto the living room couch into Brandon's arms. It wasn't long before the rain started falling outside—and the passion began "raining down" inside.

****

Watching the sun disappear behind a hilltop, Brandon and Terri couldn't be more at ease. They had found in each other everything they'd been looking for in a mate and were eagerly anticipating the many blessings the future would hold for them. Unfortunately, when they stepped off the boardwalk that night and into Terri's bed hours later, it would be the beginning of something very, very wrong!

Saying vs. SAYIN'

Buried between truth and lies exists an inside out, upside down world of half-truths and half-lies; a world rife with contradictions where people are seen as a simple means to an end, and players conceal their game tight within clinched, sweaty palms in hopes the truth will never slip free to reveal their true agenda.

13

Unfortunately, daters know this "world" all too well, having swam in its oceans, climbed its mountains, and laid beneath its stars on more occasions then we care to remember. Its residents have mugged us and knocked us over time and time again, leaving us injured by their hidden intentions. Yet, we continue to visit. We call this addictive, masochistic world: Planet Expectations.

Our dating expectations can fool our eyes, mind, and heart into seeing, thinking, and feeling what we want (see: **Reality vs. Potential**); they can force us to move too fast when patience and restraint are necessary (see: **The Ultimate Find**); they can even make us suppress who we are for the benefit of others (see: **Hiding You**). While all of these paths are dangerous to follow, they share one common theme: these are things we can't blame on anyone other than ourselves because we allowed them to happen. We set out on these dead-end roads to relationship discontent. But when we run head first into that brick wall and assess the situation afterward, we usually discover not only were we the ones driving but we ignored all of the "caution" signs we passed along the way.

There is a darker, more sinister path, though; a road where we are the passengers are being driven blindly by the expectations of others. We can't see past what they allow us to see, and those few things are usually the most beautiful oases on the planet. Although the world is one big desert, we are lead to believe that it is truly covered in lush grasses, towering palm trees, and warm springs. Not so!

Player on Player

In our story, Terri and Brandon are walking parallel paths in the direction they both want to go. However, during their sharing of hopes and dreams, they are not completely honest with themselves or with each other.

Of course there are some things that we will not (or should not) share on the first date and there are things we should automatically assume about the person we are dating. We

14

generally want to keep the conversation light and not bog the other person down with too many personal details. Remember, this is just the first date.

Yet when we do begin to share things, it is critical that we paint the entire picture and not leave blank, unfilled spaces all over the canvas. When we do that, we run the danger of never completing the painting; we may never get back around to it, having moved on to other "projects." This leaves our companion only knowing part of ourselves, which can eventually corrupt their entire opinions of us.

For some of us, this is done intentionally. We leave gaps in stories, telling half-truths so that we can maintain the interest of someone else. It is at this point that we turn the date into a game. And if we are playing a game, we are doing so to win something. So, we have to ask ourselves, "What is it that we are trying to win?"

Terri and Brandon both seem to be looking for a free ride through life, and they are depending on two different methods to achieve their goals. Terri is actively pursuing a studious image that she feels will make her more appealing to a particular type of man, while Brandon is creating an image to attract a woman who will help him realize his dream.

Fortunately, Planet Expectations is full of suckers, so he will eventually find someone to fulfill his dreams for him, giving little regard to who he steps on and destroys in the process; and Terri will find her "knight in rusted armor" who will admire her for her mind and give her the world without her asking.

When we come across these types of people, we need to either run away as quickly as possible or let them walk on by. The problem is that as professional players, they have perfected their game to get what they want. In time we are able to see their intentions, but not after being taken for a long ride down a dark path.

After associating with these so-called "players," many of us are left burned and bitter. These are the individuals that can make dating a really horrible experience. The more time we spend in that world of leeches and piranha, the stronger we build the walls around us. But that doesn't necessarily mean we learned our lesson. Instead we may retreat or make it harder for other people to get close to us. But avoidance isn't the answer to any of our problems. Until we learn how to identify these characters and how to deal with them, we will always return to Planet Expectations like fallen angels.

So, how do we identify these players? How do we separate the real from the fake? Unfortunately, we can't! If someone has spent their entire lives perfecting their game, like a true professional, they will most likely succeed at it.

This is one of the main reasons why it is bad practice to have expectations when we date, for lofty expectations create forced fulfillments. Take the time to get to know one another. Be honest about who you are and what your intentions are. Don't bring a list to the table; bring a listening ear instead. That's what the dating process is for.

We don't know where Terri and Brandon's path will go, but they've both taken the first step on the wrong one, for sure. Their intentions easily fed into the other's expectations, filling each other up with false hopes and empty promises. We only hurt ourselves when we allow our expectations to be taken advantage of by someone who's hiding their intentions. Be smart. Don't give them anything to manipulate. Enjoy the date for what it is and listen with your ears *and* your heart.

To The Point

- Dating is filled with "half-truths" and incomplete pictures
- The dating world is filled with the hidden intentions of people looking to fulfill their own selfish fantasies; don't be that person's "sucker"

- Lofty expectations may place you on other's destructive paths
- Don't bog down early dates with too many personal details, but when revealing, paint the entire picture
- Don't let the cruel behaviors of these people affect your interactions with future dates
- Take your time in getting to know potential mates
- Give honesty and expect honesty, but don't expect everyone to be honest
- Leave you expectations at home and bring your full attention, instead, on a date

A Better Move

Don't hide your intentions when getting to know someone. Be honest and give the other person the chance to decide if they are willing to play along.

Contemplative Corner

1. What are some of the signs you've noticed when someone is trying to play you?
2. How have you justified ignoring these signs in the past?
3. What gaps do you tend to leave when sharing personal details?
4. What details have you discovered later about potential mates that eventually altered the course of the relationship?
5. How has giving too many personal details on early dates proven to be destructive for either you or your date?

Kara & Matt

Kara and Matt connected like the Transcontinental Railroad, finding the completion of a long journey in their union. Both known as notorious daters, they were viewed by their friends as two people who had found their match in one another, and excitement in both camps helped to fan the fire of Kara and Matt's mutual admiration.

****

It took a total of eight dates for Matt to consider exploring a possible future with Kara, even though things turned a promising corner during their second night out. Matt had been waiting for a woman to say one phrase to him for a very long time: "I'm willing to have a Menagé-A-Trois, if that's what my husband wants...but only for my husband!" When he heard that statement, Kara, with her open mind and desire to please (yet good girl sensibilities), separated her from the rest of the pack.

Kara, on the other hand, had really enjoyed the upbeat rhythm of Matt's personality. A nouveau renaissance man, as she liked to call him, Matt seemed to be a jack of all trades and had his hand in a number of different ventures. When he wasn't running off to real estate, e-commerce, or various other sales meetings, he was surrounded by artists at café houses and open mics where he played guitar and recited his poetry. She knew that it wouldn't be soon before Matt would be a superstar. And it sure didn't hurt that he was a fantastic cook as well.

****

With his fingers rattling away on his PC's keyboard, Matt had begun the arduous task of breaking the hearts of the many other women he'd been seeing. He wanted to get to a point where he didn't have to turn off the ringer when he was with Kara, so he knew he had to let his bourgeoning new status be known. Hoping he'd made the right decision, Matt released a heavy sigh as he clicked "send" on his screen, transporting yet another email to an unsuspecting admirer.

Across town, Kara was preparing for a date she'd scheduled two weeks ago with an old friend she hadn't seen in a while. As she sat in front of her vanity mirror, guilt started to rise in her belly because of what she'd seen as Matt's developing intentions, but the memories of good times with Donald helped to quell her shame and regain focus on the evening's events. The mixed advice from her roommates Jill and Monifah sought to inflate her sense of confusion, but Kara was able to block out their debate as their heated words shifted from her to each other.

****

Donald's frisky behavior may have been viewed as inappropriate in the elegant Mexican tapas bar, *Alejandro's*, but Kara didn't seem to mind. Holding the door open for his beautiful companion, Donald felt a hard pinch on the side of his butt cheek (retribution for an earlier incident where he goosed Kara's behind with both hands). He grabbed the hem of her orange, pleated skirt so that it would rise as she walked. Feeling the air rush along the side of her thong, Kara's feet brought her entire body to a stop. She tugged her skirt from between Donald's fingers and gave him a playful, but deadly look of lustful revenge.

Alejandro's was packed for a Monday night, and the wait for a table was 40 minutes. After putting their names on the list, both Donald and Kara announced the need for a restroom break. Having spotted their locations, Kara led the way, and pulled Donald along by his tie. Making their way out of the direct sight of the other patrons, Kara unzipped Donald's fly and reached into his pants. Donald grabbed her by the shoulders and pulled her into a corner besides the men's room for a kiss.

The restroom door swung open and startled them both, but Kara never removed her hand from caressing Donald's manhood. As the chef exited the restroom and squeezed past them, they returned to their make out session only to be interrupted once more—this time by the sound of her own name. It was a waiter, who so happened to be Matt. At least now she knew why he always smelled like refried beans.

Hiding You

Have you ever found yourself laughing at a date's joke that wasn't funny? Or even describing yourself as something you knew was far from the truth? Maybe you wore a long weave, grey-colored contact lenses, eyeliner, lipstick, a short skirt, and a pair of heels that hurt the hell out of your feet when you really preferred to rock your cropped 'do, go "au natural", and sashay around in your Bohemian skirt and flip-flops instead? Anyway you spin it, you were not being true to who you are, and you were not allowing your date to see the real you.

We wear masks all of the time and there are very few people in our world who have witnessed our full collection. We are not necessarily trying to disguise who we are, but instead mask ourselves to fit various situations. The masks we wear at work are different from the masks we wear with friends; and the masks we wear around our kids are different from the masks we wear around our own parents. (I mean, who can forget the first time you saw your strict, stern parents being chastised by their *own* parents?).

Only a fool believes that "keeping it real" means refusing to *ever* wear a mask. If that were true, then we've all been "keeping it real-fake" our entire lives, figuratively speaking of course. Because we all know wearing masks is a part of life, since it is simply expected depending on the situations we find ourselves. What you do Saturday night at that club, you wouldn't think of doing Sunday morning in church. That's out of respect—and common sense. Hence, the mask.

However, that line gets smudged into a shadow of varying grades when it comes to dating. For some reason, we go beyond just wearing a mask and put on an entire costume. Why is it that all of a sudden we become afraid of showing who we really are? Do you ever notice when you really like someone that the costume becomes even more elaborate and heavier because it is adorned with layers of sparkling objects to distract the curious eye from seeing what's really there?

Who Likes Me, Who Doesn't?

There is a very amusing dynamic that exists in the dating world that may not exist anywhere else in our lives: the people we like don't necessarily feel the same way about us and the people we could care less about are absolutely crazy about us. We wonder how this can possibly be; why can't "Tara" see the things in me that "Donna" can? It is because of the different masks we wear with different people.

When we are interested in someone, we wear the mask we think they will like, drifting further and further away from who we really are; when we are not interested in someone, we give no thought to donning a mask and therefore show them exactly who we are. There's no surprise which "you" will be more attractive since everyone loves a person who can be "themselves." So the real question is what mask are you wearing around whom and how can you switch them so that who you like likes you and who you choose to keep as "just a friend" feels the same?

When we are faced with this particular circumstance, we don't simply switch the mask, we create new ones. These masks are also true reflections of ourselves, but the poorest, most vial impressions of who we are. Because we want this one person to like us, we become what we believe they will find attractive. That's when we begin changing our wardrobe and our hair; our sense of humor and our attitude; our eye color and our behavior. We exude false confidence.

On the other hand, we do what we can to make ourselves less appealing to the people we don't want. Instead of being our well-groomed selves, we may skip out on the shave and a haircut. We become distant in conversation and snippy when the other person says things that annoy us. Basically, we look for ways to sabotage that person's experience with us. And if we play our cards right, the person that will be left standing is the one we wanted all along.

The Other Me
Now that we've ridded ourselves of that person who didn't peak our interest and have taken up with the person of our dreams, it is time to start a brand new life—a life based on a bastardization of our true selves. But we are happy and that's all that matters, right? Wrong!

The problem with this new situation is that now we are stuck with the daunting task of having to keep up that fallacy. We now have to continue wearing that hot, heavy, shiny costume *plus* the mask every time we are around this person. That means laughing at their corny jokes, eating their mother's horrible Hotdog Ravioli, and taking golf lessons.

It is only a matter of time before the costume becomes too heavy or too hot to wear anymore. Those shiny little adornments will tarnish, break, or fall off. Staring at that mask in the mirror will eventually bore us to nauseam, and we will start to suffocate beneath the layers of lies. It all comes down to seeing how long we can lie to ourselves, because as long as we do, we can maintain the lie to the other person.

We can hide as much of ourselves as we want, but the truth is too strong a force to remain hidden forever. When it finally comes tearing through our costume and mask, the pain we will experience when we lose that person we lied to will be a thousand times more painful than had they never been a part of our lives.

The Energy Factor

When we find ourselves in the company of people that we really like whether it is our friends or family members, our energy is higher than normal. We feel a tinge of excitement in our spine. However, that same energy that serves to energize some can easily repel others.

Those people who we find that really enjoy our company have at one point or another felt our energy (like electrical currents), felt that vibe of ours and plugged in our groove like a socket. And as we discover this, we are either not interested in that person or we may not feel that person's vibe so much, we lower the voltage; we become what is know as being cool.

If the person has already plugged into our energy and they haven't unplugged by the time we start cooling off, it is like leaving a baby hungry. They crave our energy, which makes them appear to like us even more. It is not so much that they have any greater feeling for us; it is that they are looking to plug back in...to feed their hunger. So, their energy changes, increases. It is like trying to start the engine of one of the first cars with a crank, where they expend more energy trying to reconnect with ours. The further away we pull that energy, the faster they run to try to catch it, until we get tired of pulling and we change our energy. It becomes negatively charged and we feel forced to hurt their feelings.

Unfortunately, this is sometimes a necessary step to detach them from our energy because they were unwilling to do it themselves when we pulled away. We just need to be careful how much negative energy we give back. Are we trying to shock them like when touching a metal handle after walking across a shaggy carpet, or are we playing Zeus and trying to strike them down with thunderbolts?

Our actions around someone we really like are not too dissimilar from those that were portrayed by the people that wanted to be with us. That energy is usually over the line. We become so excited to see them that if they were plugged into our energy, we overheat them or we burn them out. The force is so great, it actually takes on the characteristics of negative energy to where you become repulsive.

So the solution, it would seem, is to lower our energy when we have the pleasure of being around the person we like. Don't be so hungry for their energy; become cooler. That doesn't mean being something that we are not that can result in Karma making an appearance. It means sharing less energy; finding a balance between showing our affections and not scaring people off.

You will hear me make this point several times in the book: Our society encourages us to be excessive. We can't just have one drink and have a good time; we have to consume and consume until we are drunk. There aren't a lot of matters in life that call for this kind of excessiveness and showing our interest for someone definitely is one of those times. Learn to be like a Jet from "Westside Story" and be cool, man...be cool!!

Behind the Mask In Front of You

Within this realm of mask wearing and costume changing, there's another side that we often come to regret later on: not seeing what's really in front of us. There are times when people are wearing a certain "face" and we ignore it because we see what we are looking for as opposed to what's really there (see: **Saying vs. Sayin'**), but what I'm speaking of is not being allowed to see the person in front of you at all.

As we have seen, people will momentarily, and I stress *momentarily* (even though that moment may last a few years) change who they are because they believe it is what's ex-

24

pected or needed to capture us. They dress themselves in the costumes and wear the masks they believe we need to see to accept them better. They aren't just fooling themselves if they think that's what we need; they are fooling us because we think we are getting the real deal. That strips us from our power to choose because when masks are worn we actually have no idea *who* we are choosing.

However, we also do ourselves a disservice because we will allow that costumed person into our lives so quickly. Instead of taking the time to really get to know someone before we start making commitments to them, we accept the mask that we see and hold onto that image, believing this is who they are and this is the person that we've been waiting for all our lives. We are so anxious to fill up that space that we aren't always aware of what we are filling it up with.

In the story, Matt believed he was getting a good girl with a hidden, freaky side. Even though he was careful not to rush into a physical relationship with Kara, he already decided she was going to be the woman that he would court. Therefore, he began making changes based on who she presented to him; not who she really was. If he hadn't seen her at *Alejandro's*, he probably would have eventually discovered that he had a wild woman on his hands, but would have believed she was only wild with him.

Kara was also fooled, but by Matt's ambitions instead. She enjoyed the fact that he was so talented and involved, and she was confident that he was going to be a star one day. What she couldn't see was that Matt was completely unfocused; a so-called "Jack of all trades, but master of none."

We meet many people who are driven and talented and seem to have a plan that is sure to lead them to success. We'd love to ride their coattails as far as they will take us. They sell us dreams as easily as candy, but the dreams aren't always so sweet although it may look absolutely delicious.

We have to do a better job of giving things time to develop because just as it is said, "time will heal all wounds," it is also said "all things will be revealed in time." If you embrace the latter quote, you won't find yourself having to deal with the former.

The Question that is *Not*

The most useless and *pointless* question a woman can ask in dating is: "Where do you see this going?"

As we'll discuss in a later chapter, dating is not an investment. So, if you are dating someone only with the specific hopes that it will lead somewhere, you are missing the whole premise of this book and I advise you to start reading from the beginning again.

The reason why that question truly is *pointless* is because when a man is ready to be with you, you won't even have to wonder. That man will make his intentions known and he will court you. When he does, he will come fast and hard to sweep you off your feet. If you feel the need to ask that question, that means he hasn't laid out his intentions, which means he either hasn't made the decision yet or he isn't planning on courting you. If you ask that question prematurely, you could blow any chance you have of being courted by that individual.

So, relax and just enjoy the moments as they come, because once again, "All things will be revealed in time!"

To The Point

- We tend to wear masks that fit into particular situations; every circumstance can't handle the "full" you
- It's easy to hide who you are from potential mates, particularly when it isn't even necessary
- The different masks you wear may have the reverse effect than you desire
- We tend to be our true selves with people we aren't genuinely interested in

- It can be hard to continue wearing the mask after it has had it's desired effect
- Once you give someone a taste of what they want you may find it hard to get them to let go of the relationship, depending on that person's reaction
- When genuinely interested in someone, show a little restraint as to not overwhelm them
- Try to see someone for whom they are, not for whom you would like them to be
- Be prepared for someone to remove their masks
- Don't be so quick to accept a person for what they first appear to be; give them sometime to reveal their true selves to you
- Let yourself see where things go instead of asking, "Where do you see this going?"

A Better Move

Take the time between relationships to discover who your "true self" is, so that you will know in advance who it is that you are presenting to potential mates.

Contemplative Corner

1. Name three (3) situations where you knowingly wear different masks
2. In what ways have you distorted a part of your personality or physicality to appeal to a potential mate?
3. At what point, in past relationships, have you noticed people begin to let their masks slip?
4. In what ways have people demonstrated more of an interest in who they think you are instead of who you truly feel you are?

5. When in this situation, why has it been so hard to let go of the other person when their interest in you waned?

Anthony & Camille

As Camille yelled at her mother on the phone, Anthony shook his head in disbelief and wrapped his lips around another fork full of mac-n-cheese. He never understood how a woman could be so disrespectful to the person who gave her life, but be so sweet and caring to others who meant so much less. He decided to dismiss it as just another one of the many anomalies in Camille's complicated personality.

One thing Camille was really good at was multi-tasking. She could balance a ruler on her nose while playing hopscotch and singing the theme song to "The Wiz." When Camille saw only one bite of her homemade mac-n-cheese left on Anthony's plate, she took it to the kitchen to refill all the while continuing to berate her mother. She knew that the creamy dish was Anthony's favorite and all she cared about was making sure he was satisfied.

Anthony couldn't help but watch Camille, with her sexy, voluptuous behind bouncing delightfully in her white sweatpants as she walked into the kitchen. He thought it was unbelievably cute when she got so fiery; she even walked with attitude.

Camille returned from the kitchen with Anthony's plate piled high, steam rising into the air from the noodles covered in hot cheese, but no telephone. He figured Camille's quest to borrow more money from her mom had ended unsuccessfully, which meant he was headed for a night of The Big Three C's —complaining, cursing, and crying. He didn't mind though, because Camille was always a more passionate lover when she was upset.

****

29

Another Monday morning had arrived, and Camille continued to lie in bed—like a sack of rotten potatoes—complaining about not wanting to go to work. Having dropped out of college right before the start of her senior year so that she could make some *real* money, Camille had been stuck working as a temp for over four years. She was beginning to realize she made a mistake and planned on returning to school in the fall.

But spring hadn't even sprung, and Anthony, as he prepared for his long day of work as a correctional officer at a juvenile detention center, had to once again remind her that she still had to make ends meet until then. After much prodding from Anthony, Camille made her way into the shower, and eventually off to her assignment.

****

Even though they'd only known each other a few months, Anthony felt like he'd really helped Camille get on the right track to pull her life together. When her mother tossed her out onto the street three weeks prior, Anthony was overjoyed to take Camille in until she could save enough money to rent her own place. Having been so completely taken by the strikingly beautiful young woman, Anthony was convinced that she was *The One*, and there was nothing he wouldn't do to make the budding relationship work.

****

It was after two o'clock in the morning when Anthony heard the keys rattle in the locked door. When the top lock turned, Anthony was sitting completely erect although he was still hazy from having fallen asleep on the couch. Camille stumbled into the house drunk and gassy. When she saw Anthony staring angrily at her and before he could get a word out, Camille sucked her teeth and reminded him that he was neither her man nor her dad.

Anthony didn't utter a word. Instead he just sat and watched Camille stagger through the living room, tripping over the rug, and falling head first into the wall. Camille disappeared behind the love seat, landing on the floor with a thud, and released a loud fart, which made her laugh. When she pulled herself up, she noticed Anthony still wasn't speaking.

She asked him to say something, but he didn't. She pleaded with him to make a sound, but he refused. Feeling like she was about to push him over the edge and ruin the one good thing she had going, Camille scrambled to her feet and tried to manage the sexiest walk possible with her intoxicated body. She dropped at Anthony's feet and begged his forgiveness. When he didn't budge, she decided to reach deep into her bag of manipulative tricks and began kissing him, seductively, yet drunkenly, on his forehead, on his neck, on his broad, bare chest, on his stomach, and continued downward....

****

As the sun began to reveal the light of day, Anthony was woken by the smell of French toast and sausages. Dreary eyed, he meandered through his apartment to the kitchen, but not before observing how immaculately clean the living room was. When he entered the kitchen, the first thing he saw was Camille's wide hips swaying to the music on the radio as she flipped the French toast cooking on the stove. The only thought Anthony could form was how great of a mother she was going to make for their kids one day.

Reality versus Potential

"Who are you going to believe...me or your lying eyes?"
--Groucho Marx

31

We live in a very superstitious society: black cats; splitting poles; the number thirteen:

- "Don't break that mirror. You'll get seven years of bad luck!"
- "Don't throw your hat on the bed. You'll have bad luck!"
- "Don't marry a musician. He'll break your heart!"
- "Don't swim right after you finish eating. You'll drown!"

We are conditioned to believe in what could be instead of dealing with what is, putting us in a position of looking forward blindly. This kind of thinking can have both positive and negative affects on our ability to function and thrive within this world.

We are taught to think about tomorrow so we can prepare today; understanding that we will be held accountable for our actions and our inactions. It is essential to the social order that we recognize the consequences of living only for today. These lessons are meant to keep us safe in the absence of laws and logic.

Because so little meaning is placed on these lessons, a number of people (particularly those belonging to a younger generation) quickly abandon them and live strictly for the moment. It is only after being beaten down by the harsh realities of life do they begin to understand the cost of living "footloose and fancy-free."

On the other end of the spectrum, there are quite a few people who forget all about living for today (i.e. enjoying the moment). They plan everything and everything is a work in progress. They have goals set for every aspect of their lives, whether it is getting a promotion or getting into heaven, and they are afraid that if they do enjoy life too much, they may lose focus, get off track, or even burn in hell.

Once again there is no balance, and there's nowhere this is reflected better than in dating. Either people are out to get what they can get and not worry about the consequences of doing so or they are constantly planning, trying to figure out how to make one date turn into a lifetime commitment. Both ways of thought do share one similar trait, however: the selfish fulfillment of one's own desires.

A date should be both selfish and self-less. We want to have a good time but we want to show our companion a good time as well. That's the balance.

Faith in the Faithless

This superstitious upbringing has another downside: not seeing things for what they are; the reality of the situation. How many mirrors have we broken? How many poles have we split? How many black cats have crossed our path? If our luck has been bad, more than likely it hasn't been because of any of these reasons. The reason our luck is usually bad is because of the way we live our lives and what we bring into it.

We sometimes welcome unhealthy matters into our lives with open arms, holding them in our grasp and absorbing them like a virus. Our faith in our ability to change things that we have no control over is strong—and dangerous. We let these creatures infect our world because we believe that our love is the pesticide, but that toxin is poisonous to us too.

A few things we neglect to learn before we've caused ourselves unnecessary pain is that we can't love anyone more than they love themselves, and we can't believe in someone more than they believe in themselves. This falls in the same category as not being able to be truly honest with someone if we can't be truly honest with ourselves.

There's a natural order in life where certain phenomena must take place before a particular happening can occur or be fulfilled. How can we ever expect to have a healthy and fruitful relationship with that special person when we don't even have one with ourselves? So many of us seek out relationships to fill our own voids, like everything we are missing can be found in someone else and once we are with them we will be complete. Since when does one plus one equal one? Are we to assume that we haven't progressed past the constitutional definition of the slave class? Are we still only three-fifths a person? Maybe we are only two-fifths and we are looking for that three-fifths in someone else so we can become one!

This incomplete character that we see in the mirror is all that we recognize of ourselves. Of course there's more to us, but we haven't gotten to know those parts yet, and sometimes we don't want to get to know them; we'd rather remain ignorant of it or ignore it because the work that will be required to fix or change those things is too much.

When we start down the path of a relationship with two-fifths of our person still hidden away, we aren't allowing our potential mate the opportunity to experience our entire flavor. They think they are getting a light-n-sweet cup of coffee, but the espresso has settled to the bottom of the cup and will slowly turn the drink bitter. As we get to know ourselves better, so will our companion and the stronger our unions can become.

We will grow and change continuously throughout our entire lives, but natural, gradual growth and taking an active part in knowing ourselves better are two different things. We don't know what experiences we will come across in the future that will aid in our growing process; that's beyond our influence and control. But getting to understand who we already are and being willing to deal with what it is that we discover is within our sphere of control. All it takes is reflection, honesty, and desire.

This is defined as *self-actualization*, which leads to *self-acceptance* and ultimately *self-love*. Because knowing ones self is to love ones self, and no one can love us more than we can. But no one can truly love us if they don't really know us, and that takes knowing ourselves first.

Unfortunately, people who can't be honest with themselves about themselves will likely not be honest with themselves about other people either. They will be exposed to all of the flaws of an individual, but only see or accept the parts of that person they feel is necessary to the completion of their mission. Those are the people who welcome the viruses into their systems; people like Anthony, whose mission is to settle down and start a family.

Camille is like the face of a pubescent teenager with all of her imperfections and blemishes on display for the world to see, but all Anthony sees are pretty eyes and a beautiful smile. He figures that in time the "acne" will either go away on its own or he can show her how to "cleanse" herself from it. But no matter what he does, if Camille doesn't think there's anything wrong with the way she looks, she is not going to do anything about it, and Anthony will be stuck doing "skin care" for a long time.

It is fantastic that he has the ability to look past someone's surface and see a deeper beauty that's waiting to reveal itself, but sometimes we have to accept that what we see *really is* what a person *really is*. We can't ignore the reality of what *is* by putting our faith into what could possibly *be*, especially when someone shows us time and time again that they are fine with the way things are. As a wise person once said, "When a person shows you who they are, believe them."

Just as we have to accept ourselves for who we are, we must do the same for others and allow them to make whatever changes they see fit in their own time.

To The Point

- In dating, it is important to exist in the world of "What Is…" as opposed to the world of "What Could Be…"

- Balance preparing for tomorrow while living for today by enjoying every moment and recognizing the consequences of your actions and inactions
- To achieve the proper balance of selflessness and selfishness on a date, or in a relationship, find joy in showing the other person a good time
- Be accountable for your own "bad luck" by recognizing the unhealthy circumstances you welcome into your life
- Loving someone more than they love themselves and believing in someone more than they believe in themselves can often lead to painful situations
- Achieve a sense of wholeness with yourself instead of looking for someone to complete you
- Get to know and become comfortable with as many aspects of your character so that you can share all of your with someone else
- If you can't be honest with yourself about yourself, how can you expect to be honest with yourself about someone else
- You can't force anyone to change, especially if they don't see anything wrong with themselves
- Accept someone for who they are, where they are, when you meet them, and don't be swayed by their "potential"

A Better Move

When you find yourself with a toxic person, no matter how much potential they may show, let them go. It's better to be alone before you are infected by their toxicity, than to become toxic too and eventually find yourself alone, anyway.

Contemplative Corner

1. In what ways have you been caught up with someone's potential when overlooking the person that they presented to you?
2. What situations have you allowed to take root in your life even though you suspected they may not be healthy?
3. In what areas of your life have you looked to others to fill in order to achieve a sense of wholeness?
4. How have you tried to change someone, or hoped they would change, to fit what you were looking for?
5. How do you go about trying to find balance in making yourself and someone else happy?

Karen & Jeff

The darkness of Karen's lonely apartment seemed less morbid than usual when she removed her key from the lock. She closed the door with a bump of her hip, fastened the three locks, and began the long process of removing her four-inch heeled, knee-high boots. She loved that Jeff towered over her despite her added height; she could still feel the imprint his lips left on her cheek as he bent down to kiss her goodnight. His gentle touch caused her skin to come alive with goose bumps.

The end of a wonderful date had come way too soon as Karen reflected on the many laughs and obvious chemistry she shared with the tall, beautiful man whose name missed matching her own by a single vowel and a single consonant.

The plush beige carpet felt like clouds beneath Karen's aching feet as she sauntered to the bathroom, removing her sexy eveningwear with each step. Completely naked, other than the light-blue, lace panties she bought specifically for a night like the one she'd just had, Karen stopped to grab her cordless phone and pour herself a glass of red wine before running herself a bubble bath. Jeff's air of sophistication made her feel like a woman of great distinction, and what better way to top off the night than with an aged Merlot, a bath surrounded by fragrant candles, and soft jazz while she waited for his call.

Karen slid her panties down her muscular legs to the bath mat and slipped into the soothing, warm waters of her copper tub. She placed the phone on the floor within arms reach so could grab it at her leisure. With a dampened washcloth folded neatly and placed across her eyes, Karen lied back and took a sip of wine. The mellow taste and thoughts of Jeff's big hands stimulated parts of her she longed for him to touch as she waited for the phone to ring so she could hear his deep husky voice and complete her fantasy.

Instead, the bath water turned cold while she continued to wait for his call.

****

Not wanting to seem too desperate or too available all morning, Karen gave into her curiosity around lunchtime and sent Jeff a quick e-mail. She couldn't understand why she hadn't heard from him. Senseless questions plagued her mind and she wondered if something might have happened to him on his way home the night before. Karen's anxiety only intensified as she spent the remainder of her afternoon checking her inbox repeatedly for a reply that never came.

****

After having placed several calls to his cell phone between the drive home and bedtime, Karen finally received a return call from the mysteriously missing Jeff as she lied sleeplessly between her flannel sheets. She could do nothing to mask the excitement in her tone when she heard his voice. His baritone "hello" had put her restless mind at ease and her entire body at attention.

The two exchanged simple pleasantries before they discussed their respective days. Although she wondered what took him so long to call back, Karen didn't want to be rude and ask; she was just overjoyed that she was speaking with him at that moment. She did question the difference in his conversation, though, but Jeff simply attributed it to exhaustion.

Before the chat could go any further, Karen felt the need to let Jeff know what a wonderful time she had on their date. Her voice danced happily as she recounted each blissful moment from the night before.

Jeff conveyed a similar feeling, triggering a wide smile to break out across Karen's face. She sat up in her bed, cleared her throat, and asked when he'd like to go out again. Startlingly, her overzealous question was met by icy silence.

Hesitating, Jeff searched for the "right" words to inform Karen that although he enjoyed himself, he didn't feel any great chemistry between them and didn't feel a second date would be necessary to convince him otherwise. When he finally let his thoughts spill, they flowed with the force of a river set free from a broken dam, and crushed Karen's emotions undertow.

After bidding her a good night, Jeff's voice disappeared into the darkness with a *click,* and Karen remained upright in her bed, stunned. It took her a long time to fall asleep as she tried to figure out what she missed on the date that he saw—or didn't see; thoughts that woke her the next morning and forced her to stay in bed an extra hour still wondering.

No 2nd Date is Ever Guaranteed

A date can be a wonderful experience, filled with all the delights of a dream and all the possibilities of the future. There are so many opportunities to show someone a good time; all it takes is decent conversation brimming with depth and sincerity, a fine location, and no pressure to please one another.

It is such a simple concept; one would think that we all experience phenomenal dates on a regular basis and bad dates were seldom, if ever, had. But good dates are like meteor showers, fine and rare; and a great date is like a comet streaking across the sky, outshining the moon. That's just how infrequent they can be. Instead, our dating experiences almost always force us to have some sort of expectation: to have a decent to poor time or to find our future husband or wife.

When that great date comes along, we cherish it like a family heirloom. After sifting through all of muck and mire, we finally stumble across a little nugget of gold, and we want to stake our claim! This is where we will plant our flag and build our fortune.

Jeff was Karen's nugget of gold. We can easily imagine how Karen's dating life had been prior to Jeff if she is anything like us. The piles of dirt she had collected on her shores stood shoulder to shoulder with the surrounding mountains. However, she endured and thought she had found that one gold nugget, as her reward. It would be silly for her not to be excited; but she should beware of *fool's gold*.

One Date at a Time

After a wondrous date, we often allow the excitement to get us all worked up. We start writing our names side-by-side, plotting a course to the altar, picking out his and her towels, and naming the kids—all in our minds, of course. We start *exhaling* all over the place, hoping it will settle us down and get us focused on attaining our life's goal of starting a family.

This is true for both men and women, because we've all been sucked into the "gold rush" and are infected with its fever. Dating has become a treasure hunt and we have to find something of some value before our tools get rusty.

It is easy to get ahead of ourselves and anticipate the next outing. Our desires are inflamed, sparked by the possibility of being pulled to safety after falling over board into the shark infested sea of loneliness and despondency. We believe to the core of our waiting souls that we have found what we've been looking for—our true love (see: **College Courtships**)

But one date has nothing to do with love and everything to do with infatuation (see: **The Ultimate Find**). And the one thing that ruins most first dates is not having our expectations met. So what can ruin a second rendezvous after a successful first date…allowing our expectations from the first date to influence our behavior and conversation during the second.

We all need to feel good about ourselves and our experiences, but we have to be careful not to let our emotions take the place of logic. We must cherish the experience, not the person, because we don't have control over what happens next.

Mutual Satisfaction

Events from a truly special first date will play over and over again in our minds. We will always have that first time etched in our minds as a standard, so even if we are let down by the second date, we will give it another try convincing ourselves we can duplicate that initial "high." (see: **Hiding You).**

That can be quite dangerous, leading us into an unhealthy addiction. But if all we have is the memory of that first time without having a chance to experience it again, we could either stress ourselves out wondering why we can't duplicate it or turn into a zombie stalker, trying to find that person that can help us achieve it.

The fact that maybe we were not meant to experience a second date with a particular person never enters our mind. If we had a great time, we expect that our date had just as good a time, if not better, as well. And according to our conventional wisdom, heavily influenced by our shallow expectations, our date absolutely should have no reason to deny us a second date. Unfortunately, that's not always the case.

Everyone reacts to certain stimuli differently, so the things that we may have found to be sensational may have only affected our date mildly or, possibly, had an adverse effect on him/her. Let's take conversation for example. We may have thought our dialogue was scripted by a master screenwriter, but our date thought the banter was childish and pointless. Or maybe we thought the discussion was so wonderful because we were able to dominate the whole conversation and talk about ourselves. The problem is everyone doesn't want to hear about just us. They would much rather *join* in the conversation (See: **The Bad Date**).

We have to be very careful to distinguish the reality of the situation from what we want the situation to be (see: **Reality vs. Potential**). So many times we say that we are feeling a certain vibe or chemistry, but the feeling isn't mutual. That's when you must ask - was it really a vibe we felt or was it our bad prior experiences influencing our expectations?

With Karen and Jeff, it appears the feelings were not mutual. It is possible that Jeff met all of Karen's criteria for a good possible mate but she didn't meet his (see: **The Interesting Chick**). That doesn't mean that there's something wrong with Karen; we just need to realize that everyone isn't meant for us, despite how we may *think* we feel about them, and we shouldn't lose any sleep over it.

Karen obviously took something away from the date that Jeff didn't. This doesn't mean he didn't enjoy himself, but there was something about Karen that just didn't make his heart sing like he made hers. There was something missing from their interaction that Karen didn't see. Maybe for Jeff it was just an average date and there was nothing so special about it that he saw a need to go out with Karen again. We will never know for sure, but Karen will have to live with Jeff's decision.

Let's not carry our baggage from our past into each new situation. It is really only the moment that matters in a date. The past will help add structure to our future relationship when we find the right one, but there's no sense in worrying if that future hasn't been written yet. While we are so busy worrying about what could be, we often forget to enjoy what simply is.

A Good Time, but not a GREAT Time

There's something that we need to ask ourselves after a fair or good date. Although we may be looking for that truly GREAT experience and PHENOMENAL chemistry, do we feel it necessary to continue dating someone if we are convinced no possible future committed relationship would occur?

If we have a good time with someone, then we simply have a good time. Period! There's nothing wrong with establishing new friendships, especially if there are things we have in common with the other person. Jeff may have enjoyed himself with Karen and he could have easily continued to do so if he hadn't written her off so quickly. As long as both parties understand that the relationship is platonic, a fruitful friendship can easily emerge.

Also, anyone can have an off night. One date really doesn't give us a true opportunity to fully learn about a person. Unless it was a particularly awful date, we should be open to going on a second date to confirm or rebuff what we experienced on the first go around. Everyone deserves a second chance!

To The Point

- It's easy to become overly excited after a great date, but that's where you need to control both your impulses and expectations the most
- One great date does not guarantee a successful second date, or a second date at all
- Not all mutually shared experiences are experienced the same way
- A person has the right to deny you a second date
- Just because you desire someone doesn't mean that they are meant for you to have
- Be prepared to accept disappointment and rejection when dating
- Remember to be in the moment on a first date, and not let past experiences or future expectations influence your behavior

Tariiq Omari Walton

- Be willing to give a second date, even in the first wasn't perfect; anyone can have an off night!

A Better Move

Enjoy the date as it is happening. Afterwards, try to control your expectations for the next date to save yourself from a bigger disappointment. You don't have to prepare yourself for the possibility of happiness, but you do have to be ready for a possible let down.

Contemplative Corner

1. If ever, how have you felt pressured to continue seeing someone when you knew it would lead no where?
2. What expectations tend to arise in your mind after a truly great date?
3. What reasons have people offered for not wanting to go on a second or third date with you?
4. What occurrences have you experienced on a date that your date interpreted differently than you?
5. How have poor past dating experiences affected either your thoughts or actions on a first date?

45

Ryan & Alana

There's nothing like finding that special someone in an instant. Ryan and Alana shared this view of one another after their first date; a first date that neither wanted to ever end. They held the same contempt for foolish games, the same love for church and God, and the same longing for a family. The vibe was so strong that their eternal foundations shook when in the presence of one another. Destiny had brought them together; *soul mates* finding each other through a storm of failed relationships and dashed hopes.

Recognizing they had both finally found everything they ever wanted in one another, they agreed over the telephone one night that there was no need to look any further. Each had volunteered to stop seeing other people immediately, and even discussed the possibility of moving in together. They wanted to wake up to one another every morning, sharing the warmth of the sun and bathing in its light.

Ryan was so excited after he and Alana got off the phone that he could barely sleep. He tossed and turned, repeatedly sliding his hand over the empty spot on his bed that he knew would soon be filled. Across town, however, Alana slept better than she had in years. Her satisfaction was so great, it was as if she'd just finished Thanksgiving dinner at her grandmother's house and the "itis" was setting in. Alana's dreams were filled with rainbows, music, and sunshine that night.

Since he was renting on a month-to-month lease, Ryan found himself carrying garbage bags stuffed with his clothing into Alana's apartment three weeks after their first date.

****

Alana had never met someone so desperate to satisfy; Ryan catered to her every desire. She never had to ask for anything because whatever she needed, he'd gotten her. He use to keep his place immaculate, and now that they were living together, he would even get up to clean her house while she stayed in the bed. He wanted to show her that he was serious, and Alana believed him.

This was no one-way street. Alana always wanted to pay when they went out, and she was always willing to go wherever Ryan wanted. Being the artistic person that she was, she often drew pictures of her man and wrote poetry of her love. Ryan would find new, exciting creations all over the house on a daily basis. After a while it became a game: find the new symbol of Alana's love today. Because Ryan was always cleaning up, it was never too hard for him to do so.

****

Having the opportunity to spend so much quality time together, Alana and Ryan both received an overdose of each others annoying habits. The more time cruised by, the more they could see how much they weren't alike, but they agreed they were *soul mates* so they had to make it work!

Even though it was just his habit to be tidy, Ryan soon found that he was the only one cleaning. Not only did Alana usually stay seated on the couch while he straightened up around the house, but it was her mess that Ryan was usually cleaning up. He tried not to nag, but he couldn't help himself. The first major fight they ever had was over the two dirty glasses Alana left in the living room while Ryan was in the kitchen doing the dishes.

Alana quickly became annoyed with Ryan's anal-retentive ways. She was a free spirit and her surroundings reflected that, but Ryan always had to have order and that drove her crazy. She even started leaving things, like the infamous dirty glasses, around the house on purpose to push Ryan's buttons.

But what bothered her most about her new found circumstances was that she always got stuck doing the things that Ryan wanted to do, and he always wanted to do the same boring things. Where Alana was into concerts, poetry readings, and museums, Ryan was into bowling and playing pool. Even though she enjoyed those things too, she recognized that there was much more to life than what Ryan was open to experiencing.

Plus, Alana began to see why she was often the one paying for everything—Ryan stayed broke!!

****

Two stressful months later, Ryan found himself at the doctor's office. He woke up three days later with abnormal bumps and blisters on his genitalia that were causing him great discomfort, which he was careful to hide from his live-in girlfriend. He wanted to be sure he knew what his affliction was before he told Alana.

The doctor confirmed Ryan's greatest fears: herpes.

The Ultimate Find

There are many things in life we get overzealous about. Think about that last semester of school before graduation. We get so distracted with "Senioritis," we often end our academic careers on the worse possible foot.

What about when we were children? Remember being so excited on Christmas Eve that we could barely sleep, and then woke up way too early for our parents liking? How about when we finally had enough money to move out of our parent's home? We were in such a rush to move into our own space that we didn't even bother to consider sticking around for a few extra months so we could save enough money to buy our first home instead.

Overzealousness is as much a part of growing up as pimples and braces. It is natural to get excited about moving onto the next phases of our lives, and in doing so we often over look some simple realities. For Ryan and Alana, they forgot to get to know each other before making a commitment to one another and sharing a residence.

Building before Settling

All relationships need time to grow, and it is through careful attention and nurturing that this process happens. Even a house needs to be completed before it begins the settling process, and that may take a considerable amount of time depending on the strength of the foundation and the type of land it is being built on. Nothing in a relationship is instantaneous other than infatuation.

Infatuation can be a powerful and confusing emotion. As stated in the introduction, it is frequently confused for love, and because of this, we often find ourselves making forced decisions that should naturally be realized when it is indeed love. Infatuation will trick us into skipping the necessary steps that lead to a "successful" courtship and relationship, ultimately heading into an abyss of sorrow and regret.

The easiest way to determine whether it is love you feel for someone or if you are simply caught in the rapture of the moment is to inject *time* into the equation. If the butterflies are fluttering their wings in your stomach after knowing someone only a day or two, you can bet your life it is a pile of infatuation you've stepped in. Love at first sight is an over-romanticized concept that's usually only mentioned when you reflect on the early stages of your relationship during your 50th wedding anniversary.

Building a relationship around the emotion of infatuation is like using mud instead of cement in the construction of a foundation. Sure it'll dry hard, but it washes away easily and

49

won't hold up to the pressure and weight of the structure being set on top of it. Taking the time to get to know each other is the cement, and there's no substitute for time. Without that, you might as well be building a house of cards on top of a line of dominoes.

A Price to be Paid

Of all of the regretful occurrences that happen to us in life, the hardest to live with are the circumstances where we could have practiced better control. Those are the ones that we face every time we look in the mirror, making us question what our state of mind was at the time: the "what the hell was I thinking?" questions; the "I should have known better!" insights.

If we are blessed with the good fortune of asking these questions of ourselves for only a brief period of time, we got off lucky. Looking at their story, the reality of Ryan and Alana's decision to come together as quickly as they did could have resulted in potentially life-altering/life-sabotaging consequences for both. The living situation can easily be remedied when Ryan finds his own place. They may feel only a short bit of time was wasted in that regard; easy to heal from and move on.

It is the more dreadful results of such a hastily formed union that can last a lifetime. There's nothing like having a child with someone you aren't very fond of (see: **Waiting Too Long**). But it seems that Ryan and Alana will be facing something even worse: a viral disease for which medical science has no cure.

We don't know who was the original carrier of the herpes virus or who infected whom, but this is one of the most unfortunate circumstances that can arise from establishing such an association. We don't have to necessarily move in with someone for them to infect us with a disease that we'll suffer with for the remainder of lives; all it takes is exposure during sexual intercourse. But by taking time to get to know someone

50

you give yourself the time—and courage—to ask the hard questions; questions that must be answered because although herpes is incurable, it is not deadly. However, there are many other viruses out there that are.

These are the some of the most regrettable outcomes of being irresponsible with your actions and decision-making. Love is indeed hard to come by and even harder to keep, but the last thing we want is for the hollowness of an infatuation to be the cause of so much physical and emotional turmoil. Let time do its job so that we have more of it to enjoy without it being obstructed by our ignorance.

To The Point

- Nothing in a relationship should be instant, other than infatuation; healthy relationships should be nurtured and given time to grow
- Don't confuse feelings of infatuation for feelings of love
- Infatuation is often the cause for impulsive behaviors you may later regret
- There's no substitute for time in matters of relationship development
- The consequences for impulsiveness in affairs or relationships may be greater than the experience was worth

A Better Move

Get tested for STD's before engaging in unprotected sex, and ask that your partner does, as well. Tests don't exist for all STD's, so you may not know if you are putting someone else's health at risk until it is too late.

Contemplative Corner

1. How has being impulsive left you in a situation you could have otherwise avoided?
2. When has being impulsive been worth the resulting consequence?
3. How do you know when you're feelings are genuine versus just being infatuated with someone?
4. Have you ever confused someone's infatuation for you with their genuine feelings?
5. How have you dealt with the consequences of impulsiveness?

Brandi & Troy

Brandi's doe eyes brightened as the young man approached her table. Maybe it was her drunken state or the club's darkness, but she didn't remember Troy being quite so fine. With his gaze fixated on her, she felt glued to her seat, forcing Troy to lean over to give her a hug.

Before Troy settled into the booth and placed his napkin across his lap, Brandi excitedly asked about his day. Her notable interest, along with her luminous smile and even more radiant eyes, aroused Troy's own curiosity about Brandi. Having grown use to women who liked to dominate the conversation with shallow desires and hollow successes, Troy found Brandi to be a breath of uncontaminated air.

Confident, yet a bit nervous, Brandi ordered a second glass of white wine. Troy had already seen how wild Brandi could get when she had a few drinks in her and became excited at the possibilities the evening could bring. He knew she was an easy mark and asked the waitress to bring an entire bottle.

But Brandi was on her own mission. Every question she asked was followed by another; probing deeper into Troy's life and thought patterns. By the time they ordered their meals, Brandi had recorded the names of each of Troy's siblings into her brain, as well as his place of birth, his job description, his salary, his net worth, his future career plans, and what he had for lunch that day. Troy never got a chance to redirect Brandi's questions because she had a new one to ask before he could finish answering the last.

****

Two bottles of wine and a second helping of the never-ending pasta dinner special, and the tone of the conversation had become loose, loud, and frank. Brandi had been able to get Troy to break one of his main first date rules and speak openly about his desires for marriage and children. He usually saved that kind of talk until well into the courting phase of his relationships, but between the whirlwind of alcohol and the long line of questioning, his walls had toppled.

With her alcohol buzz removing her inhibitions as well, Bradi also felt much freer to ask questions that would normally be taboo for any first date: questions about sex. Troy obliged her and told all about his sexual escapades in—and out—of committed relationships. He even revealed secrets about his reoccurring sexual dysfunctions that had caused the deterioration of numerous affairs.

Unfortunately, the no-holds-barred level of honesty brought Brandi crashing down from her drunken high. Disgusted, she attempted to change the subject, but Troy was on an intoxicated roll and, with his hopes still running high with the possibilities of him and Brandi getting a little naughty later, stayed on the sexual theme. What he failed to realize, however, was that with every honest, yet candid word he said, he was pushing Brandi closer to the exit door.

****

The bill came while Troy was away in the restroom relieving himself of the contents of their three shared bottles of Pinot Grigio, and Brandi quickly paid it hoping she could slip away before her young, erectile dysfunctional, drug-needing date returned. Just as she took her coat off of the brass hook on the side of their booth, Troy happily trotted around the corner.

Feeling like the prison escape tunnel she'd been digging for three years had just collapsed on top of her, Brandi turned around to let Troy help her with her coat. As he lifted the coat to rest on her shoulders, Troy brushed his pelvis against Brandi's rear end to let her know what he had on his mind.

Walking out of the restaurant two steps ahead of him, Brandi was not sure which nauseated her more: Troy's awful attempt at enticing her or the fact that he never asked about the bill. Before they reached her car, Troy grabbed Brandi by the wrist and spun her around for a kiss. But she snatched her wrist away and cocked her fist at him in defense. Troy laughed apologetically before asking Brandi if he got the job.

Not Finding any humor in the situation, Brandi let Troy know she didn't think he'd make a good fit on her team. Without even a simple "good night", she hopped into her car and sped off.

Application Denied!

A Date *Is Not* an Interview

Being on a date gives you a good opportunity to learn more about a person as well as a few things about yourself. You may discover your likes (plump lips and southern accents) and dislikes (crooked teeth and sweaty palms). Basically, the more you date, the more you'll learn about yourself.

The main objective is to experience different levels of chemistry and find out how to better establish relationships. But a single date is like the screen on your camera telephone; it is to capture a "snapshot" of your companion for the evening. Unfortunately, we have the tendency to turn the date into a picture show, replete with slides and headshots. We want to see how well the person performs in comparison to the standards we have set.

So, we seek to get as much information out of them as possible at one time. It becomes less about enjoying someone's company and more like conducting a candidate search. We might as well have an application and a contract in hand, and a tape recorder on the table.

Remember: A DATE IS NOT AN INTERVIEW! It is not a treasure hunt (see: **No 2nd Date**). If we act like we are on a fact-finding mission, then we are essentially breaking the cardinal rule of dating: expecting too much too soon. We have to ask ourselves what good will all of this information do us if this is our only date?

Who's who?

In our story, Brandi was successful in getting Troy to reveal things about his life and personality that saved her from having to experience it unnecessarily first hand. She didn't have to wait to be in his bed to discover his "problem," and she also didn't have to wait until he captured her heart only to have him break it anyway.

Her investigation saved her from a lot of stress in the long term, but did she give Troy a chance to show her a good time that night? Her one date with him wasn't about tomorrow; it was supposed to be about that night. Brandi instead sabotaged what could have been a fun evening by spending it planning for tomorrow.

At the same time, Brandi only got to know Troy's inebriated side of the story. If he had been more focused, he would have told her about all the stress his ex-girlfriends had put him under that kept him from performing well in bed. He might have also informed Brandi that since he and his ex-girlfriends had agreed to "open relationships," he technically hadn't cheated on them. Unfortunately, Brandi's rapid-fire questioning during Troy's inebriated state lead her to make assumptions about issues that may never have affected her, especially since it might have been their only date.

Who Are You?

Another drawback of playing detective and keeping your date under the spotlight is that we neglect to share things about ourselves with our date. A date is never meant to be one sided. Sometimes people suffer from severe "loquaciousness" and won't shut up; other times they may suffer from "lockjaw" and not have a word to say; and then there are people like Brandi who choose to keep all of the attention off of themselves by placing it on their dates.

This can be viewed as questionable behavior for other reasons beyond what we've discussed. Is it possible that Brandi is attempting to hide something about herself? Is this a way to keep the ball in her court so that she has the power to direct where the future of their interactions will go?

In an attempt to uncover the imperfections of other people, what we are really doing is hiding our own flaws from them. We spend so much time trying to get to know who they are and what they are about, we don't give them a chance to get to know the same about us. Brandi was able to soak Troy dry of information before their main course, but from what we see she didn't give him the same satisfaction.

This style of interaction is on par with doing all of the talking and not giving our date the chance to talk about themselves (see: **The Bad Date**), which can be construed as rude and inconsiderate. Interviewing can also make our date feel uncomfortable and cause them to not share things once they pick up on the game that we are playing.

If this behavior is a power move to maintain control, this too is quite unfair, especially considering a date isn't a time to vie for power. It is not a political campaign where we keep our opponent off balance by forcing them into a defensive position. Neither our dates nor our mates are our adversaries. If it is a relationship that we seek, we achieve this by building together, not tearing each other down to stay on top.

A date is an optimal time to share things with someone new. We want to learn enough about someone so that we can determine if we would like to move forward with them, and we want to give them the same chance to make that determination about us. The reason why we have the friends that we do is because we like who they are unconditionally. They may do things we don't always agree with, but that doesn't necessarily make them bad people. Why wouldn't we give our dates the same benefit of the doubt?

Understanding Ourselves

We are not letting Troy off the hook in this situation either. His conduct was very distasteful, as were his intentions and expectations. He looked at Brandi as a target; someone he felt he could easily have his way with based off of their initial meeting.

We have to be careful of what message we are sending people when we carry ourselves in certain ways. Drugs such as alcohol and ecstasy can minimize our inhibitions. When function under their influences, we can easily portrait ourselves as something we normally wouldn't when we are sober and in control.

Alcohol in this story put Brandi in danger and it also saved her. Her conduct under its influence showed Troy how easily he could take advantage of her. At the same time, the alcohol caused him to reveal some of his most unattractive characteristics that opened Brandi's eyes to his true intentions.

An important thing to remember while dating is to relax and have fun, but to always be in control of ourselves. We are free to lose our inhibitions when we are with someone we know has our best interest at heart, but not with someone we barely know. As with so many other things, time will show us who we can trust and who we can't, but when we don't let time play its part, we can be setting ourselves up for more harm than temporary fun is worth.

To The Point

- Don't treat a date like a treasure hunt

- Even though an answer to a question may be correct, it may not be totally accurate
- On a date, be willing to share as much as you ask of your companion
- A date is a great time to share various thoughts and experiences with someone new
- You should learn just enough about someone, on a date, to determine if there will be another date; not someone's complete life history
- Be careful of your alcohol consumption; a first date isn't the best time to be completely uninhibited
- Relax without losing your self-control

A Better Move

If you are compelled to ask questions on a date, ask questions that provoke thought and stimulate conversation. Also, make sure the questions somehow relate to your own likes and interests.

Contemplative Corner

1. How has being inebriated made you more attractive to someone on a date?
2. In what ways has someone made you feel interrogated on a date?
3. What questions would you find hard to answer on a first date?
4. What have you learned about someone on a first date that helped you determine whether or not you would go on another date with them?
5. Why do we sometimes feel the need to control the flow and the tempo of early date?

Edgar & Joi

Joi threw her hand over her mouth to keep from spraying her whiskey sour over everyone at the table. She knew better than to put anything in her mouth when her friend and co-worker, Tiffany, was telling a story, since she always said the most outrageous things at the most inappropriate times.

Happy Hour at the *Red Room* was a Friday night tradition for the group of five ladies sitting around the oak coffee table. Resting comfortably on overstuffed chairs and sofas, Joi and her friends toasted to the end of the work week and engaged in a game of "Pick Their Profession", cracking jokes on whomever they thought deserved it.

Before Tiffany could unleash another round of offensive tales about some of the evening's patrons, she paused mid-sentence to absorb the vision of beautiful masculinity that had just pushed his way through the double mahogany doors with a petite sista on his side. When each of the ladies looked up to see the ebony prince that had captured Tiffany's attention so intently, they let out a collective sigh. Expecting to see a hideous creature dressed in argyle and spandex, Joi turned around just in time to catch his gaze. When their eyes met, his smile quickly faded

As he walked his companion to an empty pair of stools at the bar, his female admirers shared fantasies with one another that they'd like to fulfill with him. The only one who didn't comment was Joi. Instead, she stared blankly into her empty glass, wishing the ripping feeling in her chest wasn't her heart breaking. After four dates, three of which ended with a splendid night cap, Joi hoped that she was building something meaningful with Edgar. Now she knew the truth.

Lost in thought and drowning quietly in her emotions, Joi didn't even notice her friend's growing excitement caused by their approaching dream man. Edgar stopped just as he reached Joi's shoulder. A panic ensued when she felt his overwhelming presence hovering over her and she pretended not to hear him calling her name over the thump of the deep house music emitting from the over-head speakers.

Edgar placed his hand on Joi's shoulder and leaned into her ear to be sure she heard him. Joi felt herself melt under the weight of his touch but fought the urge to shrug his nasty mitts off of her. She didn't trust where his hands might have been recently.

Responding to the unfettered gasps of her friends, Joi finally acknowledged Edgar's presence and mustered a fake smile as she turned to say "hello." After a few forced pleasantries, Joi knew she had to introduce the gentleman to the crew of friends that seemed to be so taken by him. Each woman swooned and cooed as Edgar made his way to each of them, shaking their hands and asking their names. Joi watched him closely, wondering if it would be unladylike for her to dig her size eight heels into his lower back.

After introducing himself to everyone, Edgar announced he had to get back to his lady friend, but offered to buy a round of drinks for what he called "the sexiest group of women he'd ever seen in the Red Room." With stars in their eyes and smiles on their painted faces, Joi's friends gladly accepted his offer. He wished them all a good evening and winked at Joi as he walked away.

Naturally, a barrage of questions followed Edgar's departure. Joi tried to mask her discomfort about what had taken place and paralyzed her friends when she revealed Edgar was the man she has been bragging about for the past two weeks.

Seeing Joi's obvious grief over what she had discovered, the crew of lovely ladies sat quietly for a moment with nothing to say. That was until Tiffany broke the frosty silence with the proposition that Joi ask Edgar if he'd be interested in a threesome with her and his beautiful companion, damning if she would let the young woman have him all to herself. As the ladies laughed hysterically at Tiffany's statement, Joi was plagued with a burning question:

Would Edgar still be taking her out for their planned lunch the next day?

Your Date's Date

A series of dates can hold a lot of value for a person in search of a relationship. It means that someone liked you enough to go out with you on more than one occasion, which implies that they probably see something worthwhile in you. You hope for more and start to build expectations. But you forgot one thing: to ask the person you are dating if they are seeing anyone else.

When we first meet someone and exchange information, we often assume the person is single. You figure they must be if they are making plans to get to know us better. Why would anyone with a girlfriend or boyfriend be interested in seeing us again if they already have someone at home? As we attempt to answer this question, it would be wise to remember that a lot of seemingly good people do cheat. But in those cases where the person isn't being a selfish, two-timing mutt, it is important to be mindful of the meaning of the word *single*.

As was discussed in the introduction, "single," in its simplest terms, means to be "unmarried;" but in its more practical application, the meaning is expanded to include not being in a relationship. Anything beyond that would have to be discussed by the two parties involved if they want to fully understand each other's status. However, it is often much easier for us to assume than to ask.

We don't want to seem too intrusive when we are just getting to know someone, especially if we are not to have expectations. And then our egos interfere and start to corrupt our logic. Many of us believe that it doesn't matter if the person is seeing someone else because after one date with us, they won't have a need or a desire for another! We are again fooling ourselves.

We don't know anything about that person until either we ask or they offer the information to us, and a number of those topics (which we'll call *The Unspoken Insurance*) aren't always comfortable to discuss. In our rush to find someone or move through all of the various relationship stages, our *Unspoken Insurance* gets its most use. Our *Unspoken Insurance* covers things such as: our dating status; our rebound status; our employment status; our political affiliation; our financial status; our religious/spiritual beliefs; our criminal record; our sexual orientation; and most of all, our medical history.

In our scenario, it is obvious that Joi made at least one major assumption about Edgar. She presumed that she was the only person Edgar was dating, and instead of finding this out in private, it was unfortunately revealed to her in front of her four friends. Is this because her ego interfered or was this just one of those things covered under the *Unspoken Insurance*?

It is actually because of our ego and our ability to bathe blissfully in ignorance that we hesitate to find out some of the fundamental and most important aspects of our date's life. In the world of dating, it should always be assumed that your date is seeing at least one other person, unless that individual informs you that they are not, and that they are—by the strictest definition—"single." This will help you to maintain your level of expectations and not over-romanticize the circumstances surrounding your date. When you allow your expectations to surface without being properly informed, the degree of disappointment can compare to that of being lied to.

If Joi assumed that Edgar wasn't seeing anyone else, then it is pretty safe to surmise that she believed she was the only person with whom Edgar was sharing his bed. We don't know for sure that Edgar and his date that evening were indeed engaging in a sexual relationship, but it is better to assume than to find out the hard way. Not only is it better, but it is smarter and safer.

No, thinking that we are not the only one does nothing for our egos, but it can potentially save our lives. Not knowing a person's relationship or health status can lead to a lot more than heart break. It can lead to you being stalked by the person whose mate you are sharing or to a venereal disease (see: **The Ultimate Find**).

Now, let's take this one step further. If someone has sex with us on the first or second date, you might do well to assume that he or she has done so with others. This essentially means that our bedmate knows about as much about the other person as they are seeing as they do about us, which is practically nothing.

There's so much we really don't know about a person after the initial series of dates, much less after the first two. That's why it is crucial that we have honest and frank discussions with the person before we decide to have sex with them. We'll get into the concept of "sex making a relationship" later in the book, but for now it is essential that we understand the pitfalls of that "blissful ignorance" we enjoy so much.

It doesn't seem as though Joi and Edgar knew each other or their sexual history or current dating status well. For them, their *Unspoken Insurance* was cashed in that night, and they hopefully parted ways unscathed. However, that "premium" could have run pretty high if either found out later that a disease was exchanged or a baby was conceived.

To The Point

- It's okay to ask your date if they are dating or seeing anyone else

- You're fooling yourself if you think someone will instantly stop dating other people because they went on one or even a series of dates with you
- Don't assume to know the answer to any question you haven't asked
- Unless explicitly stated, always assume that your date is dating other people
- If someone sleeps with you on the first or second date, you can assume you're not the only person to have experienced the matter
- It is possible to have honest and frank discussions without seeming to pry
- "Blissful Ignorance" has no place in the development of a relationship

A Better Move

This is a hard topic to broach early in a series of dates, without seeming intrusive or full of expectations. But one should definitely have the conversation, with the person they are seeing, as the budding relationship begins to turn more intimate. And be prepared to make a difficult decision if the answers run contrary to what it is that you want.

Contemplative Corner

1. What questions do you find hard to ask someone when you first meet?
2. How have you been affected when you found out that you were not the only person involved with someone you really liked?
3. What things have people you were dating wrongly assumed about you?
4. How did the truth affect the relationship?

5. How would you react if you saw someone you were dating on a date with someone else?

Eric & Vivian

Eric stared at the green numbers on his car's dashboard with wide-eyed wonderment. Being 20 minutes late for his first date with Vivian made him a little nervous as he shifted the car's gear into park. In his mind, a woman as professional as Vivian would probably be pretty upset that he hadn't called to say that he was behind schedule, and her mood could dampen the entire evening. When he thought about all the money and grief he could avoid expending by simply putting the car into reverse, Eric remembered the curves that outlined Vivian's sexy outfit when they first met and quickly reconsidered his position.

As the early Thursday evening stars twinkled behind him, Eric rushed up the path to Vivian's huge townhouse and pressed the door bell with his thumb. He paced restlessly as he waited for someone to answer the door, but no one did. He pressed the button again and took a step back to see if there was any movement in the well-lit home.

When a shadow appeared in one of the upstairs windows, a mild sense of angst began to tumble about in Eric's belly. He reminded himself to calm down, but by the time the door opened, he was even more nervous. But his anxiety settled once he discovered that Vivian wasn't ready after all. Only half of her thick head of hair had been curled and her face was totally absent of makeup, making her appear older than Eric remembered.

Vivian ran back up the stairs as Eric made his way into the foyer. Walking up the stairs behind her, Eric apologized and tried to explain why he was late, but Vivian brushed it off and asked him to wait in the den while she dressed.

67

Nearly forty minutes passed before Vivian made another appearance. Walking into her den, she found Eric fast asleep on her gray, brushed leather couch with his shoed feet on her marble coffee table. Before he could get in a good snore, she woke him with a pillow to the head.

****

Chéz Modéle, a little Parisian restaurant in the heart of Morganshaw, was dimly lit with candles and heavily decorated with pictures and sketches of fashion models across the ages and across the world. The dark, cobble stone walls created a majestic feel, like dining in a 14th Century castle. Walking a few steps behind Vivian as the maitre d' lead them to their table, Eric noticed the tailored suits worn by the restaurant's male patrons and the pink-labeled bottles of champagne sitting in sterling, ice-filled bucket stands beside many of the tables. He checked to make sure he had his wallet.

Eric removed his jacket and sat down at the table while, only a few feet away, the maitre d' pulled out Vivian's chair and helped her slip out of her coat. By the time Vivian took her seat, a throbbing migraine was already taking residence in Eric's balding head; the open menu in his hands was the reason. He had no idea what Palette d'Ail Doux was or why a plate of it with Red Mullet costs $45.

Having spent her junior year of high school as apart of a student exchange program in Marseille, Vivian ordered from the menu with the fluency of a wine taster from Bordeaux. Eric enjoyed hearing Vivian's French accent so much, he asked her to order for him too. But when she engaged the garcon in conversation in his native tongue, Eric knew she was only doing it to show off.

Vivian babbled on throughout dinner about her vast travels, her college years, her family plans, and her career goals. She didn't even notice that Eric had stopped listening to her two hours earlier. His attention was constantly being stolen away by the short skirts and the thigh-high stockings worn by the restaurant's waitresses, who all could have been models in their own right.

After being motioned to, the garcon stands the billfold between Eric's cup of coffee and the small desert dish where his white, chocolate-covered banana crepes once sat. Vivian grabbed the bill and, with a shocked expression, offered to pay half. Without needing to see the bill himself, he gladly and thankfully accepted Vivian's gracious offer.

****

Pulling into the space next to Vivian's Lexus 300 SUV, Eric didn't even get a chance to put his car into park before Vivian wrapped her arms around his neck and brushed the side of his cheek with her lips. She reiterated the good time she had and Eric tossed her a look to suggest the evening didn't have to end. She instead left him with an impassioned kiss and exited his vehicle with of the grace of Ingrid Bergman boarding the airplane at the end of *Casablanca*.

Eric waited just long enough to see Vivian pull the keys for her townhouse from her tiny, red leather purse before he began to pull off. Glancing up to see her waiving him down, he pulled the car back into the space and waited to see what she wanted. Vivian sprinted down the path to the parking lot, motioned for Eric to roll down his window, and asked him why he wasn't coming in.

The Bad Date

As we have seen, the dating world is a very confusing and sometimes terrifying place, so it is important to date well. In order to do that, there are some basic rules—a code of conduct—that you might consider first.

So, what do you do on a date? We've already established that having expectations can lead to a disastrous evening out, and we recognize that there really is no point to a date other than to have a good time, but how do you go about making that happen?

Well, let's start at the beginning....

Confirmation

It is crucial to think of a date as an important business meeting, in some respects. You might have had it on your schedule for weeks, but things can always pop up that are of a more pressing concern. Your meeting may have to be rescheduled or postponed, or it may have to be cancelled all together. Keeping that in mind, remember the same may go for your date as well.

This is why it should be common practice for you to confirm your date. Do this the day before or even the day of the actual date, and don't wait around for the person you are going out with to call you. No, you don't want to seem desperate, but like any other meeting, you want to be sure that it is going to take place at the scheduled time. If not, you need to know before hand. Remember, you have a busy life and you need to make good use of your time.

Be On Time

Time is always a factor in dating. In the story, Eric suffered a great deal of anxiety because he was running late for his dinner with Vivian. He knew he was in the wrong, which caused him to worry about how his tardiness would affect the rest of the date. Since it is natural to be a little nervous before a date anyway, why add to the stress? Be courteous and make the proper phone calls.

Eric could have saved himself from his feelings of paranoia simply by picking up the phone to let Vivian know he was behind schedule. He probably knew a half-hour before he was supposed to arrive at Vivian's home that he was going to be late, but he didn't bother to call. Even if he called her five minutes before the original date time, Eric would have been in a potentially better position. Vivian still may have been upset that he wasn't going to be there when he said, but that's beyond Eric's control. He can only control his actions and his best action would have been to call.

The absolute wrong thing to do is not call at all. Calling after the time is even better than not calling at all. Although this can still be viewed as inconsiderate, not placing a call at all is down right disrespectful. Vivian would have been completely right to be angry with Eric—if she'd been ready, herself!

Being Ready

Sometimes it takes a while to get ready, especially when you are trying to look our best, and it is easy to miscalculate the time you'll need. That's understandable. But Vivian's tardiness was inexcusable.

As the person being picked up, you often watch the clock, hoping that your date will be late just to give you that extra bit of time. So, you find yourself fretfully hurrying through your process when you could easily call to tell the person to come a little later or for them to expect you not be ready when they arrive. It is just the considerate thing to do and consideration goes a long way. Remember, the point of the date is to have a good time. Don't ruin that good time with rudeness.

Congeniality

How you interact with your date is the most significant element in dating. Again, the only point in dating is to have a good time and show your date a good time as well.

A man must be chivalrous from the beginning of the date to the end. Now, let's break this term down for those of you who don't quite understand the concept. As a man, you should go to the door and ring the bell to signal to your date that you've arrived. Don't sit in your car and toot your horn expecting her

71

to respond like Pavlov's Dog. Show her and her neighbors some respect.

Once inside of her home (only if she invites you in), you should be the first to the door when leaving so you can hold it open for her. Then you wait for her to walk through and you follow, even if she is the person locking the door.

The same happens when you get to the car. If she is driving (which she shouldn't be doing on the first date unless you don't have a car or it is in the shop), then you hold the driver's side door open for the lady. If you have a remote to unlock the doors, you still make the effort to open the door for her, and you are not to leave until she is settled in her seat. Then you close her door.

When you arrive at the restaurant, you open the car door for her; you either walk side-by-side with your date or you let her take a slight lead; you hold the door to the restaurant open for the woman; you help her remove her coat; you hang it up for her; and then you pull out her chair for her to sit down. Never let her do these things herself and if the maitre d' attempts to steal your shine, tell him or her that you have it under control. If you are shown to a booth, then you wait until your date sits down before you slide into your seat.

At the end of the date, get out of your car and walk your date to her door, and don't leave until she is safely inside her place. Sitting in the car and waving out the window is not only tacky, but it is also unacceptable.

Although Eric went to Vivian's door as he was supposed to, he lost points later by not pulling out her seat at the restaurant, not waiting for her to sit down before he did, and not walking her to her door after the date was "seemingly" over.

Many men may wonder why doing these things are so important. Well, it is because every woman you meet should be treated with the same respect you would show your mother or grandmother. You cater to your date in the same manner you would care for the most important women in your life. It is not a question of whether this person holds any particular value in your life; by simply being a woman, she holds value and should be treated accordingly.

Being congenial also includes the art of conversation. All too often the conversations we have are weakened by our selfish roles in them. Many of us will dominate a conversation leaving little room for our date to share his or her story. When we do give them the opportunity to speak, we aren't really listening. Instead, we are formulating our next statement in our heads. By doing this, we are showing our date that we don't care; that their thoughts and their words hold no value to us.

Vivian showed absolutely no interest in Eric's life, thoughts or feelings. Maybe she was nervous and the only way she knew how to deal with her feelings of anxiety was to talk incessantly. This is something you need to recognize about yourself if you haven't taken the time to do so. If this is indeed a bad habit of yours, learn to take a deep breath and relax. Ask yourself what you have to be nervous about. No expectations, remember?

Some people treat the conversation as a sales pitch. What are you selling? Your date isn't there to purchase you. That person is there just to have a good time like you should be trying to do.

However, some of us are simply too self-centered to notice and often think what we have to say is much more important than what the other person has to say. It very well may be, but how will you ever know if you don't let the other person speak? How will you ever get to know your date if the only time you've heard their voice is when they ordered their meal? Besides, who are you to judge the worth of someone else's conversation? Share the conversation. Ask questions, listen for the answer, and respond to what the person says.

In Eric's case, he showed little concern for his date but in a different way. He allowed himself to be distracted by half-naked women throughout the night. Admittedly, half naked women can distract the strongest of men, but you have to remember where you are, who you are with, and why you are there. Give all of your attention to your date; be there with them just as they are there with you. If you are bored by their conversation, then add something to it. You shouldn't allow yourself to be talked "at" because you do have something of value to add to mix, and that person needs to know it.

Paying the Bill

At the end of the night, there always seems to be a question of who's paying what, when there should be no question at all. The man always picks up the check on the first date, even if it was the woman who asked him out. Many times a woman will offer to pay half. The man must turn her down flat. It is his responsibility—his duty—to pay for the date.

Because we are talking about not having any expectations, the woman should have some money with her just in case her date fails to uphold his manly duties. If you think you may have a problem paying the bill, it is because of poor planning. Eric should never have agreed to dinner at Chéz Modéle if he couldn't afford it. True, he may not have known that the prices would be that outrageous, but in this technological age in which we live, he could have found out ahead of time and planned properly. There's nothing wrong with doing a little research, especially when it comes to how you will be spending your money. Had he done the proper research, he would have either brought enough money with him to pay the entire bill, or he would have realized that he couldn't afford it and might have suggested somewhere else—cheaper!

Don't fall into the trap of trying to be overly impressive. Again, you are not selling yourself. The only thing your date should be impressed with is how good of a person you are; not what you have, not how much you know; not what you've seen, not who you've met, and definitely not what you can buy. You are the impression!

And before some of my sistas out there get snippy at all that I'm suggesting here, I want you to know that as men, we recognize that you can do all of these things for yourself. We know you can open you own doors, pull out your own chairs, and pay for your own meals. That's fantastic if you have the ability to do so; but just because you can doesn't mean that you should have to. Enjoy the attention as long as he is doing these things for honorable reasons. Chivalry will never be outdated.

To The Point

- Confirm your date in advance to make sure it's still happening as planned
- Don't let your time be taken for granted and don't waste someone else's; be on time for a date, or at least call well ahead of time to say that you are running late
- If being picked up, call to alert your companion that you are running behind schedule and won't be ready on time
- Remember your four (4) C's: Courtesy, Consideration, Congeniality, and Chivalry
- Don't dominate the conversation; leave room for your date to talk, as well
- Give your companion your full attention and show some interest in what they are saying
- Dating conversation shouldn't be treated like a sales pitch
- What you have to say isn't necessarily any more important than anything your date has to say
- Practice the art of Good Conversation: ask questions, listen for the answer, and respond to what the person says
- The man should always pick up the check on the first date, even if the woman was the one to ask him out

- Women should always have their "just in case" money with them
- If money is short, research ahead of time to make sure you can afford where you are going
- Don't try to impress your companion with what and who you know...You Are The Impression!
- Enjoy the attention, ladies; just because you can do everything for yourself, doesn't mean you *have to*!!!

A Better Move

Pay the person, with whom you are meeting, the greatest consideration. This means to treat them how you expect to be treated. If your expectations for yourself are low, that will reflect in how you treat someone else!

Contemplative Corner

1. How have you felt when people have shown up late or not been ready for a date when you arrived?
2. How have people reacted to your tardiness?
3. What truly makes for a bad date in your experience?
4. Why is conversation such a lost art?
5. Why are chivalry and courtesy lost causes?

Nicole & Charlie

Nicole sighed with reoccurring disappointment, as she headed to Mellow Ace's Café. She hated feeling pressured, and agreeing to meet her brother-in-law's co-worker, Charlie, for a cup of coffee felt more like pain than pleasure.

It had been four miserable months since she and Mitchell last attempted to reconcile their relationship which, filled with lies and distrust for years, had failed. Even though it was a brutal feeling to be alone after having shared a bed and a life with someone for so long, Nicole wasn't sure she was ready to start dating again; her sister, Diane, believed otherwise. With the stress of the break up, Nicole had snapped at more people than twigs under a herd of elephant's feet, and her attitude was making it difficult for her family to tolerate her.

Leaving her car in the café's alleyway parking lot, Nicole rounded the front of the building and found Charlie sitting at a patio table, reading a book. Immaculately dressed in a blue, pinstripe suit, and a warm smile, Charlie stood to greet the sour-looking Nicole. Needless to say, the warmth wasn't returned.

Charlie was well aware of Nicole's recent lackluster demeanor, but was up to the challenge of showing her a good time whether she wanted to have one or not. Sitting down, he attempted to start a conversation with a quick summary of his day while Nicole buried her face in a menu. Charlie jokingly pulled the menu down from Nicole's face, but she quickly snatched it from between his fingers and raised it to within an inch of her nose. It was then that he realized the challenge was going to be greater than he imagined.

****

It's Just A Damn Date!!!

Sipping from a cup of Green Tea that she had sent back three times because of its weakness, Nicole screwed her face at every thought and opinion Charlie expressed about the state of male/female relations in urban America. Focusing specifically on what he would do if he found out his girlfriend was cheating on him, Nicole scoffed at the sentiment that Charlie would try to work through his feelings of betrayal and forgive her.

No matter how logical and well thought out his explanation, Nicole perceived it all as an attempt on Charlie's part to *seem* like a genuinely good guy. In Nicole's mind, a good guy who didn't cheat was as much a fallacy as the stork that brings babies. There was nothing that Charlie could say to convince her otherwise, so she suggested that they quickly change subjects.

The conversation shifted to music, which swiftly delved into the overwhelming misogynistic messages found in popular Hip Hop songs. Charlie played it safe and waited for Nicole to state her opinions on the matter so he could figure out how to best navigate through the discussion without pushing any of her buttons. Instead, Nicole folded her arms over her chest and asked Charlie what he thought, instead. When he couldn't turn the tables on her, he sighed and worked up the courage to speak his mind, anticipating another Mount Saint Nicole eruption. He got what he expected....

****

While Nicole delivered a sermon questioning the motives, schemes, and behavior of men, Charlie signaled the waitress to bring the check. His eyes hung heavy like a boxer's after a vicious night in the ring. He felt vile, dirty, and worn out and couldn't wait to abandon the scene and get home.

Nicole, on the other hand, felt more empowered than she had since helping to elect her sister to the school board three years prior. Her passionate soliloquy burned with the heat of a million furnaces. After years of accepting the misleading words and inactions of a man she believed never loved her, she was finally getting the chance to let a man know how it felt to be a woman. However, her actions brought a tinge of guilt to Nicole's consciousness.

Before she could offer an apology, Charlie laid $20 on top of the check and excused himself to the restroom. His defeated gape reminded Nicole of a dog who'd been beaten with a wet newspaper. Little did she know the object of her lashing was on his way through the café and out the back door!

The Bitter Dater

We all have our down periods. It is a normal part of life. Maybe it is a bad day; maybe it is a bad year. Regardless, there will always be periods of time when we are just not feeling our best. We can't help that. What we can help, however, is how we deal with those down periods.

The first thing to remember when we feel down is that we won't be down forever—unless we want to be. All things come and go with time and pain is only meant to be temporary; nevertheless, those matters can last as long as we hold on to them.

We also need to remember how to pull ourselves out of that rut; how not to allow that pain to hold on to us. The best way to do this is to prepare ourselves for the pain by recalling how we were able to reach our greatest degree of happiness while we are at our emotional peak.

There's nothing like experiencing the high that good times bring into our lives. When those times come, it is imperative to remember what brought us to that point, because no matter how much we try, it is nearly impossible to fully sustain that elevated level of bliss forever. We could unexpectedly be knocked off of our mountaintop and tumble down to the deepest valley. The view from the valley back to the top of the mountain may seem very distant.

We may be in a great deal of pain, but the journey back to the top won't be an impossible trek as long as we can find the path that got us up there in the first place. It may take some time to make it back to the summit, but as long as we follow those markers, those bread crumbs, that we left for ourselves just in case we did fall, we will get there again.

Unfortunately, many of us choose to sit in that cold, damp valley and wallow in the river of self-pity because we either don't remember where that path is, we keep looking back (instead of forward), or we are too lazy to look for it. That's when our pain can become dangerous to ourselves and the people within our circle. That danger is at its height, though, when we introduce someone new to it. Nicole and Charlie's situation perfectly demonstrates what can happen when we level bags of bitterness and insecurity on the shoulders of an undeserving soul.

Nicole was obviously still in that mode where she wasn't ready to let go of the pain. If so, that's fine. We all need an opportunity to allow our wounds to heal, and that will naturally come with time. But that process can be helped or hindered based on how we tend to those wounds. Do we cover them with bandages or do we leave the wound open and unprotected so we can pick at the scab?

Nicole going on a date so early in her healing process was like letting an infected wound ooze. She was not in a place to appreciate a good date, and going on one so early in her healing process set her back. It was the equivalent of snatching the band-aid off of a fresh cut.

Simply put, going on a date at this stage of her life was a wasted gesture on Nicole's part because all she was doing was hurting herself more. She is basically thrown herself back down the mountain by agreeing to go out with Charlie, just to prove a point.

80

And honestly, Charlie was a fool for allowing himself to be put into the position of playing the patsy in Nicole's caper. He also had a good idea Nicole wasn't ready to re-enter the dating world, but he allowed his ego to drive his attempt at heroism. Charlie believed he had the skills and ability to tear down her walls and slay the evil dragon of bitterness. His egotistic conduct and his cowardice retreat had the potential to undo whatever progress Nicole had been able to achieve up to that point. Remember, no one is so beguiling that they can enchant a wound into healing before its time.

External Influences

Pain has the ability to turn the most giving person into the most self-centered monster on Earth. When we are suffering, it is very hard for us to focus on anything else. We neglect ourselves, our families, our friendships, and our jobs; in essence, everything that matters most to us. When we are in pain, subconsciously we want others to feel what we feel; we don't want to go through that misery alone.

If there is no other reason to get back to the mountaintop, let this be the one: the damage that is done to our relationships during these periods of stress and pain can be irreparable. At the very least, they put a great strain on those relationships and turn people away from you faster than a collapsing tidal wave, and that injury could out last your original impairment.

Because we are not our usual rational selves while this is happening, others, who love us and only want the best for us will try different and creative ways to help us. Nicole's sister, Diane, could no longer take the insanity Nicole was inflicted on everyone and decided to do something about it. She hoped the date could free Nicole from her own suffering—and her family's. But Diane's "kind gesture" could have forced Nicole into a place she didn't need to be—a rebound relationship. Doing so would have been like building a house on wet sand; it would have been unstable from the beginning.

Also, being sent back into the dating field so soon could have also turned Nicole from victim to perpetrator, by inflicting all that her ex had put her through on her new beau. On a smaller level, it was exactly the path Nicole was heading down by projecting all of her frustrations onto Charlie and trying to make him pay for the sins of mankind.

Diane thought she was doing a good deed, but we aren't always rational when we see others pain, particularly when it is someone we care about. In an attempt to help them, we start making poor decisions for them as well. What we thought was help turns out to actually cause more damage.

We need to learn to step away and let the person deal with their pain in the best way—and best amount of time—they see fit until they ask us for help. There's a big difference between being "blue" and being "depressed." We all get the blues and, with time, "this too shall pass." However, if you suspect the person is going through something more clinical that could indeed be detrimental to their well being, *that's* when it is time for you to step in regardless and aid in getting the proper help.

To The Point

- On bad days, try to remember better days and strive to regain that feeling
- Don't let your sorrow become toxic and infect your date
- If in an emotionally toxic place, don't date until you are out of it; don't date until you are truly ready and can leave your past pains out of the new circumstances
- You can do yourself more harm than good when dating with open wounds
- Don't try to play "savior" and rush someone else's healing process

Tariiq Omari Walton

- Don't be pressured by other people to do things you're not ready to do; they may seem to have your best interests at heart, but they may be reacting to the misery that your misery is bringing them
- Don't project your pain onto others, causing them to suffer the way you have

A Better Move

Make sure that you are in the right frame of mind for a date. That means being open to the experience, ready to have a good time and ready to show someone else a great time. If you are under a great deal of stress, even though you may need some relief, you may be incapable of the above.

Contemplative Corner

1. How have you gone about trying to feel better in times of sorrow?
2. What's it like to date someone who is unhappy or depressed?
3. How has having a broken heart, or just open wounds, affected subsequent dates?
4. What has been the result when you have tried to "save" someone from the blues before they've had time to heal from whatever pained them?
5. How much time do you generally need between a breakup and dating someone new?

Hope & Justin

Hope and Justin met on the second day of freshman orientation at Freedom University. The Student Government Organization was hosting a barbeque in the middle of the quadrangle for the incoming freshman class, and Hope and Justin's separate crew of friends had merged. Having spent most of the evening primping in front of the mirror, Hope and her friends were late to the festivities and had missed the food. However, Justin was nice enough to give Hope his hot dog and bag of chips, and they had been nearly inseparable ever since.

Typical of college courtships, their journey was quite rocky, but the first semester was fantastic. Enjoying their newfound freedom, Justin and Hope spent more time in each other's dorm rooms than in class—and their grades reflected it. Bringing home a 2.1 grade point average that first long, winter break almost ended Hope's educational career at Freedom University, but she begged her parents not to pull her out and promised that she'd turn her grades around spring semester.

This led to the young couple's first break up, which gave Justin the opportunity to explore *other* prospects, but the separation didn't last. Hope fought too hard to get back to Freedom U. and Justin to let any campus "floozy" scoop him up. She quickly figured out how to balance her schoolwork with her social life, and performed much better academically.

However, that brief break gave Justin a taste of what he was missing; a taste he couldn't get out of his mouth. By committing to Hope so early, he hadn't taken *full advantage* of the *real* college experience. He recognized that Hope was more beautiful and had more potential than ninety-seven percent of the other women at Freedom U., but he still had to "dibble and dabble" in the beds of various young ladies around campus before he could really "settle" with her.

But Justin had to be discreet about his "creeping" since every other straight guy on campus was waiting for him to drop the ball with Hope. Every time Hope questioned him about something she heard, he denied it like a criminal on trial and made sure to treat the women on the side with the utmost respect so they wouldn't rat him out. When they did, he would deny that too and convince Hope that everyone was simply *hating* on what they had.

Inevitably, Justin got caught and the two broke up again. All it took, though, was Hope letting one of the football players "make a play" in her bed for Justin to slow his indiscretions. This led to a long period of monogamy, but it also helped Hope put their relationship into the right context: she had to put herself—and her future—first.

****

The expectation of marriage had been a mainstay in conversations with friends and family as graduation approached for Hope and Justin. All they had heard for the past three and a half years was how lucky they were to have found their true loves in college.

Even though the two had shared a great deal of love for each other, their paths were going in two different directions. Hope had already been accepted into a master of arts in teaching program at City State University, and Justin...well, Justin didn't have any foreseeable plans. External pressure was the only thing keeping them together.

****

The day of graduation had arrived, and Hope and Justin were surrounded by their respective families, all whom had become quite well acquainted over the years. Everyone wanted the "happy couple" to pose for pictures and do so with smiles spread across their faces. But all they secretly wanted was to get as far away from the other as possible. That was easier said than done since plans for dinner were pending—as was a rumored proposal from Justin.

Instead, Justin couldn't wait to announce he had accepted a job across the country in Necropolis, and Hope was literally bursting at the seams to tell everyone that she was three months pregnant—by the Director of Student Activities. The night had definitely turned into one of surprises.

College Courtships are Pointless

If no other argument is made in this entire book, let this one be it: finding your *true love* is **not** supposed to be an **EASY TASK**! Many of us are quick to complain about how awful dating is and how hard it is to find a husband or a wife out here in the *real* world. Guess what? It is not supposed to be easy, and the only reason why dating seems so awful to many of us is because of our expectations that make us treat each date as the seed that will blossom into the world's greatest relationship. Even Snow White had to live with seven hyperactive, pint-sized miners—and die—before Prince Charming came along.

The first serious mistake we make is in thinking we *must* find our *true love*. It shouldn't be a search! We are not supposed to hide ourselves away from the world and expect someone to come find us either; even Cinderella had to get out of the house and attend the ball to meet her prince. But this is not a treasure hunt, and anyone who tells us differently is mistaken.

We sell this fairytale to young people and insist upon them finding their future wives and husbands while in college since it is nearly impossible to do so afterward. Yet another conflicting message drilled into our heads when we are young (see the chapter: **Building a Stalker**).

The other problem is the misuse of the phrase *a true love*. What is a *true love*? Some people define this as being one's *soul mate*; the only person on earth that we are meant to be with. Now, life can be rough, but how evil would that be to have us search for ONE person our entire lives? What if our *soul mate* was born in a country that he/she will never leave and we will never visit? Or what if our *soul mate* hasn't even been born yet? Sorry, but that seems to be a pretty ridiculous concept.

Others aren't quite as conservative and define a true love as simply being the person that we *will* spend the rest of our lives with. These are the people who capture our hearts and never let them go. So, who did we marry the first three times if not our *true loves*? Those damn imposters!

There's a fantastic line in a movie where one of the main characters states, "You are only allowed three great loves in your lifetime!" This could be understood to mean three true loves, and in the case of this character, he had experienced all three by the time he was nineteen. If this is the case, and we do mow through all three of our true loves when we are young, then are we destined to live the rest of our lives with no chance at ever meeting someone else?

A true love, as described in the Oxford American Thesaurus is simply "a beloved or a much loved individual." We may experience this sense of love once or a million times throughout the course of our lives, depending on how much value we place on the concept of love.

But it is also important to consider that there may be no such thing as a *true love*. Interestingly, a character in another movie simply defines love as, "...what you make, and with whom you make it." So, if we are waiting to run into our true love, then we are truly waiting on the love that we create with that much loved individual to blossom and grow; not some magical prince or princess that will save us from our awful dating experiences.

Opportunity for Growth

College or simply those transitioning years, where we are beginning to tackle the world on our own, is a very interesting time in one's life. After years of wanting to be an adult (and pretending in our minds that we are), we are finally given the opportunity to demonstrate that we are ready for the responsibility. This can be a very challenging span of time because there is so much about the world that we don't know (though we swear we do) and get introduced to, and all we want to do is find where we fit in.

It is very easy to outgrow the friends we've had since pre-school over these few short years because we are learning so much about ourselves that we either didn't understand or were unaware of. We find ourselves gaining new friends and experiencing new situations that our old friends simply can't relate to. Our lives begin to go in different directions, and we may also find ourselves alone for the first time.

The new interactions that we do experience, however, are a major force in our growth and development; our getting to know ourselves. We come across a lot of characters that will bring new flavors into our mix. We have an opportunity to see what fits, and what doesn't; what we like and what we don't; and most of all, who is right for us and who isn't.

This is why dating is extremely important. We learn so much about ourselves through our interactions with other people, particularly our more intimate interactions. And that's why it is best not to be involved in a serious relationship during this period because it is so easy to outgrow someone or for the two to outgrow each other.

That's basically what happened to Hope and Justin in our little tale; after struggling to maintain a college romance, they grew apart. Instead of exploring all that college had to offer, they decided to fight against the odds and attempt to establish something very solid and "grown up" during some of the most unstable years of their lives.

In examining Justin and Hope's conduct, we may feel that their engagement in sexual activities with other people while claiming to be committed to one another was wrong. In actuality, it was their attempt at commitment that was wrong since they should have been dating—not necessarily sexing—many different people in an effort to better get to know themselves. By not doing so, Hope and Justin stunted their own growth (see: **Sex Doesn't Make a Relationship**).

Life after College

For those of us who were fortunate enough to attend college full-time and put off the working world for a while, our period of transition is extended a few more years. Yes, we definitely learned a lot about ourselves during our college career, but a whole new level of growth takes place when we transition into the *real world*. It is like watching the bud of a rose form and finding great beauty in that only to watch it a little longer and observe its blossoming into a more beautiful flower.

So many new stresses are introduced to your life during this transitional period, it would be wrong to present your *rosebud* to someone who has their own *thorns* to contend with. Enjoy this time for what it is: the freedom to explore; the freedom to just be!

To The Point

- Finding "True Love" is not, and isn't supposed to be, an easy task
- Don't treat dating as a search for "True Love"
- Be careful of how you define "True Love"
- The years between ages 18 and 24 are typically times of immense growth, brought on by experiences related to our first brushes with true independence

- It's easy to out grow life long friendships during this time, as well as budding romances
- Developing new, platonic relationships with people of the opposite sex can be difficult when in a committed relationship
- It is good to use these years as a time to explore different people and personalities
- Maintaining long term, committed relationships during this time can stunt one's emotional growth

A Better Move

Not all relationships initiated during this "transitional time" are doomed to fail. If you do pursue a relationship during this period, there is a chance you may grow together, with someone, instead of apart. But be prepared to accept the sacrifices in life that your peers may get to experience.

Contemplative Corner

1. Which childhood fairytale has influenced your approach to dating and relationship building the most?
2. How do you define "true love"?
3. Who do you know that believes they are truly with their "Soul Mate"? How do they know?
4. In what ways have you outgrown your lifelong friends during those "transitioning" years?
5. What has been the result of the relationships that were maintained during those "transitioning" years?

Wes & Kelly

The anticipation had been overwhelming, but the first thing Kelly thought when she saw Wes was that he was nothing like she imagined him to be. The picture he had of himself on StongerLove dot com must had been at least ten years old, plus he was a lot shorter than his profile stated. Nothing about him said "successful television executive" or "small business owner." Well, maybe the "small" part was accurate, as revealed by the suit that appeared to have been tailored to fit someone six inches taller and fifty pounds heavier.

Recognizing Kelly by the description of her outfit, Wes strolled over to her table like the cool cat that he knew he was, but stopped short when he realized why she only had pictures of herself on the popular dating website from the bosom up. Although she had an undeniably beautiful face, her profile listed her body type as average. Average was a serious understatement. In fact, the only thing average he noticed about Kelly was the amount of crumbs falling down her massive cleavage from the pretzels she had been eating as she waited for him.

Despite their initial disappointments, they embraced each other, igniting the memory of the many conversations they'd held via phone and internet the previous three weeks. Kelly invited Wes to sit down, and he happily accepted.

As a waitress stood near Kelly to take her order, Wes couldn't pull his eyes away from the "twin valley" that struggled to stay confined in her lavender blouse. With all of the freaky things she claimed to have done with past boyfriends, Wes anticipated cupping her two peaks with his hands and burying his face between them for hours.

Once the waitress moved toward Wes to take his order, Kelly fantasized about driving the new BMW coupe he supposedly purchased after closing yet another fantastic deal with a major television studio, and the drive they would take up the Coast with their wine and cheese basket in tow. Unfortunately, she thought, Wes would probably have to be strapped into a baby seat having not met the necessary size requirements to sit in the front passenger seat like a big boy.

Both of their seductive, late night telephone voices were noticeably absent as they tried to engage one another in conversation. Kelly's laid back telephone demeanor had given way to a chipper goofiness that forced her to constantly show off her full-mouthed grin. She couldn't even make it through a complete sentence without flashing what seemed like a thousand tooth smile.

Wes, on the other hand, looked as if he'd been sedated by a tranquilizer dart; if he reclined any more in his chair, he would have been lying on his back. Completely void of the passion he exuded during their earlier conversations, Wes' only contribution to the evening's activities was struggling to stay awake. It didn't seem like his expectations of Kelly throwing herself at him would materialize.

With the energy at the table diminishing faster than the morals at a high school dance, the food arrived to break up the growing monotony. Wes didn't think Kelly's smile could expand more than it already had, until her full rack of barbeque beef ribs were placed on the table in front of her. Licking her lips, Kelly dug into her meal, never noticing Wes pausing to say grace. Her eating rampage was reminiscent of cave men—and not the more civilized ones like in the insurance commercial either!

Luckily, the feast actually gave Wes an idea of something to talk about. Each time Kelly stuffed her plump fingers in her mouth to lick off the tangy barbeque sauce, Wes was reminded of the jellybean contests he and his siblings would challenge each other to every Easter. He bragged of how he was able to get out of going to service at church one Easter because a single jellybean lodged itself in his throat and he had to be taken to the emergency room to have it removed. Beating his chest, he proudly stated that he won the contest that year.

Kelly feigned interest and countered with a story of her own, bragging about the time she beat out seventy-two other contestants in a metropolitan-wide hot dog eating contest after sliding thirty-six foot longs down her throat. With a wink, she mentioned that there were many benefits to having no gag reflexes, and expected Wes to perk up at the sexual connotation. Instead he placed his silverware on his plate and stared sickeningly at her with a lost appetite.

After paying the check, Wes walked Kelly to her car without much to say. Before the date began, he had expectations of going home with her. But as soon as Kelly opened the driver-side door, she turned around and stuck her hand out for Wes to shake. He happily obliged, and told her it was nice to have finally met her. Flashing him her huge annoying grin again, Kelly insincerely agreed through clinched jaws.

Starting her car, Kelly watched Wes through her side-view mirror as he made his way to a pimped out, red Chevy station wagon. She surmised his new Beemer must have been at home in his garage--right next to his tricycle.

The Danger of Pre-Date Conversations

Many of the expectations we have for our dating experiences are as much a result of our conversations beforehand as they are of our individual desires. In fact, these initial conversations are the motivators that bring our dates to fruition. It is during these times when our interests are peaked enough for us to want to take that next step.

93

These conversations can range from simple introductions to all-night gab fests. Either way, it is the conversation that helps us build a rapport and familiarize us with our companion. This familiarity and shared interest makes us more comfortable to feel like we are going out with a good friend instead of a prospect with a zillion expectations hanging over his or her head.

What does it feel like to have dinner with a good friend? Is there pressure? Are there expectations? Are there limitations on what you will do or say? Absolutely not and that is exactly how we should approach our dates. But let's examine this further.

Out with a Buddy

It is a Thursday night and almost the end of a very long work week. The need to unwind is overwhelming and you can't wait to get started. While you stare at the television from the loveseat, the trailer for a riveting new suspense/thriller flashes onto the screen. You grab the telephone, dial the number of a good friend, and make plans to meet at the theater in an hour. After hitting the shower to wash away the day's blues, you hop into some comfortable, yet presentable, clothing and get on your way.

Usually at this point you are more excited about the prospect of seeing the movie than the friend. This doesn't devalue the friendship or the friend, but the excitement is placed on the actual activity and not squarely focused on the person with whom you are attending the movie.

You and the friend decide to get a bite to eat after sitting through the two-hour movie and settle on a little bistro up the block. The conversation flows like cool water on a hot day. You catch up on things and share enthusiastic opinions about the thriller you've just seen. There's no pressure to make small talk; to make you or the person anything more than what you or they are. You just talk for the enjoyment of it. There's no agenda or hidden intentions.

When you finish your meal, you hug your buddy, agree to do this again sometime, and part ways. You are not trying to go home with him or her; you are not feeling like you are owed anything; and you are not expecting to see the friend again their next waking minute. The outing was great, you saw a fantastic movie, had a genuinely honest conversation, and enjoyed great company.

Why does a date have to be anything different?

Building Expectations

As it has been stated, the expected outcomes of a date are stimulated and maintained by our desires. Instead of looking to have a good time with someone new, we build up these great expectations of what may very well be the last-first date we'll ever have with anyone. That puts a lot of pressure on the actual dating encounter before it even begins.

We also put a lot of pressure on ourselves to be at the peak of our game. The clothes, the make-up, the cologne/perfume; they all go into the marketing plan in hopes of making a good first impression. We've turned the date from a simple good time out with a potential new friend to a sales pitch. When we are in this mode, we ultimately spend more time wondering what our date thinks about us rather than trying to have a good time.

Our self-imposed expectations cause us to move away from the essence of the date, which of course is to enjoy ourselves. That alone can cause interference, but when we start our sales pitch during pre-date conversations, we raise the expectations of our companion as well.

Talking Too Much

Insecurities can play a big roll in the way we interact with other people. The tendency many times is to over-compensate for things that we feel we are lacking, so we either inflate certain parts of our persona or outright lie about ourselves. This practice only continues on the date since the process was started in our pre-date conversations.

There was a time when we used letters and postcards as well as the telephone to arrange dates, but in this technologically advanced age, the Internet has become our closest ally. Many of us are establishing these new friends through the plethora of online mediums such as message boards, blog sites, and dating communities before we ever have the chance to hear each other's voices.

This is where the sales pitches begin. Our profiles are billboards meant to grab people's attention and pique their interest enough for them to want to connect with us. Then the second phase of our marketing plan kicks in through emails and instant messenger conversations, where we exchange thoughts, opinions, and ideas. This enables us to comfortably get to know one another better before either exchanging telephone numbers, or skipping that step altogether and setting up the date.

But many of us remain cautious about how much information we give out before we decide to pass along our telephone numbers or get together for an evening out. So, we extend these conversations for a while and learn as much as we can about the other person. By the time we do meet face to face, we feel like we already know each other.

The expectation is that who we are meeting up with is indeed the person that we've been talking to all of this time. We expect them to be strong willed and interesting; we expect them to be honest and show a genuine interest in us; and many times we expect them to look just like they did in that sexy pictures from their profile and have the skills in the boudoir that they've been bragging about. We expect that this will be the beginning of a inexhaustible romance.

Not only do we run the risk of disappointing our date *and* ourselves, but we've infused way too many expectations into a situation that was only meant to be a fun night out. It is one thing to wonder what the night will bring; it is another to expect the night to bring fulfillment to all of our desires.

We've developed a rapport already, just like we have with any other friendship. Even though it may be too early to consider this individual a true friend, we need to treat our date and our experience with them just like we would with a close acquaintance. We shouldn't get wrapped up in the marketing and advertising of it all, and let what we *think* we already know about the other person spoil our one excursion. We need to learn to take it as it comes and leave it where it ends.

To The Point

- Pre-Date conversations can have as much of an effect on our dating experiences as our pre-existing desires and expectations
- Familiarity with your companion should add comfort to the experience
- Treat the date, itself, as something akin to having dinner with a good friend, absent expectations and limitations
- We tend to build up our dates as being our last first-dates ever instead of just letting them stand on their own
- Don't over prepare for a first date
- Our tendency to over-compensate for the things we may be lacking is often fueled by particular insecurities, and can cause us to behave contrary to whom we really are on a date
- Modern technology has supplied us with the means to "over communicate" without actually meeting face to face
- The profiles we establish online are treated like billboards and subsequent email exchanges can be viewed as direct marketing advertisements

- When looking at the conversations held through emails and instant messaging, these online communications are essentially dates without the need to get dressed up and have face-to-face contact
- Control your level of expectations even after a long period of online communication
- These online personas may be a total misrepresentation of the actual person

A Better Move

Having the chance to converse extensively before actually going on the date should make for a great outing. Because you have already gained a sense of each other's likes and personalities, the activity should be well planned and the conversation easy going. What should not be planned already is the date's outcome. Let the date, itself, lead you there!

Contemplative Corner

1. In what ways do you treat your date differently than a night out with a friend?
2. How do you go out of your way to prepare for a first date?
3. What parts of your persona do you inflate on dates?
4. In what ways have you been surprised or disappointed after meeting someone face-to-face with whom you're already had extensive communications?
5. How have you used technology to increase your dating potential?

Andrea & Kenneth

The infamous third date had almost ended when Andrea and Kenneth's lips finally met. Passionate and lustful, the moment stretched across the boundaries of the night and into the next morning, but that's where it ended. Andrea slipped from Kenneth's hungry grasp, opened the front door to her apartment complex, whispered 'goodnight,' closed the door, and began her arduous journey up the stairs to her fifth floor flat.

Kenneth remained on the apartment's front stoop for a minute before he realized it wasn't a joke; Andrea hadn't invited him inside. Dumbfounded, Kenneth adjusted his scarf and flipped up the collar of his coat to protect his neck from the brutal fall winds as he sulked back to his car.

Letting his feelings settle during the drive home, Kenneth acknowledged his bitter disappointment and growing anger. After an enjoyable, yet expensive dinner at the posh fondue restaurant, the Bubblin' Stew, and considering the urban legend of third dates typically leading to a couple's (usually disappointing) first sexual romp together, Kenneth figured the odds were good that he'd get a taste of Andrea's Ethiopian seasoning that night. Instead, all he got was to return to his room in his brother house and quietly relieve himself of the mounting tension that had built in his loins.

****

Sitting at his work desk with a calculator in hand, Kenneth began tabulating the combined bills from his three dates with Andrea. He had happily picked up the tabs for each one, believing it wasn't a woman's place to pay when she was on his arm. Looking at the three hundred twenty-four dollar total,

Kenneth began to wish he hadn't been so chivalrous and eager to impress his beautiful companion.

Kenneth's coworker, JD, interrupted his accounting activity when he poked his head around the corner of his cubicle to ask about his date. The excited curiosity in JD's voice quickly diminished when Kenneth tossed a look of disgust in his direction. JD instantly knew there wouldn't be any tales of ripped panties, arched backs, and pleasurable savagery he could relish in.

Still fuming over all of the cash he had dropped, Kenneth tossed the small, plastic adding machine toward JD. JD's jaw dropped when Kenneth explained that the figures reflected what he spent on three dates, where the only results were a stuffed belly and an unsatisfied craving for sexual gratification.

Shaking his head, JD tossed the calculator back to Kenneth and encouraged him to make sure he got his money's worth if he ever did bed the sensational Andrea. JD laughed to himself as he walked away, commenting that he hadn't spent half as much money on his own wife in the two years they'd been married.

Frustration overwhelmed Kenneth's senses as JD's quip reminded him of his "financial loss," and he picked up the phone on his desk to dial the number he had committed to memory. A few rings later, his ears were set ablaze by the sexy sound of Andrea's "1-900" worthy voice. Kenneth sat up in his seat and announced his name softly, yet sternly into the receiver. Before Andrea could finish telling him how much she enjoyed herself the night before, Kenneth had demanded to know when the two of them would be taking things to the *physical* level.

A riotous laugh bellowed from Andrea's end of the telephone line, disturbing Kenneth's spirit. Just as he was set to declare his displeasure with her inability to take his question seriously, a loud *click* thundered into his eardrum, followed by the lonely sound of a dial tone.

Kenneth pulled the phone from his face unbelievingly and rested the receiver on its base. He then realized he would get no *return* on his *investment* after all....

Dating Is Not an Investment

Many of us live and thrive in dual realities where we are both cautious and wasteful with many of our most precious resources, specifically time and money. These are two valuable commodities within our society and we function like schizophrenics when it comes to their use.

Think about how often we save time for ourselves only to use it wastefully. We decide not to spend Thursday night out with our friends so we can get a jump on cleaning in preparation for our parent's weekend visit. Yet, instead of doing as we intended, we spend that Thursday night catching up on all of our digitally recorded shows instead. Now we are forced to rise with the roosters so we can try and squeeze five hours on housecleaning into two. In fact, we have compounded *wasting* time with *losing* time by cutting our sleep short to fulfill the duties left undone from the night before. This is *not* a good use of time!

As often as we complain about not having enough time to make major changes in our lives or enjoying ourselves more, we'd laugh at how ineffectual this argument is if we were to add up how much time we waste and lose each week. However, we are often more cautious of how we spend our money than what we do with our time. Indeed an oddity when you consider that you can make as much money as you want in a lifetime, but you can never get time back. Yet, we are much more likely to fight someone for taking our money than taking or wasting our time.

The worth of these two resources aside, there's nothing that gets to the heart of our society more than money. If we invested as much money into creating time as we invest time into making money, we'd live forever! Instead, we place more importance on the earning and spending of our dollar bills than anything else in our lives.

Society dictates that we devote anywhere between half to three-quarters of our waking lives to *getting that cheese*. If we take into account how many hours we work in order to afford our "lavish" lifestyles (which basically means how much we can afford to spend), it is no wonder why we've become so hysterical about money.

Two major points need to be made about this pandemic. One, if we are going to dedicate this much time to work, it is imperative that we have a love and appreciation for what we do to earn that money. There's nothing worse than the feeling one has when they wake up morning after morning to go to a job they find unfulfilling. When we do this, we are simply asking to be miserable and stressed out. We need to do a better job of finding work that's fulfilling, enlightening, and enriching.

Many of us are steered away from following our passions because doing so does not always allow us to earn as much money as we want, which leads to the second point. If we are going to place so much value and spend so much time on the pursuit of earning money, we really need to begin to ask ourselves if it is worth it.

It is generally accepted that the majority of people within our *advanced* civilization aren't very good at saving money and planning for the future. We are trapped in a cycle of constantly spending what we earn. We earn it, then we spend it; then we earn some more and spend that too. Yes, we live in a consumer-driven economy that's dependent on our spending habits to survive, as has been repeated several times in this text, but seeing how we slave in jobs we don't care much for in order to make money, we should understand our deeper motives.

The Way We Feel About Ourselves

This grand culture of ours is not designed to make us feel better about whom we are as individuals. As a matter of fact, it seems as if the intention is to do exactly the opposite and cause us to feel poorly about ourselves. While we are upheld and celebrated in one spotlight on the world's stage, another spotlight is later *shined* on us to show us all that we are not indeed as special as we would like to believe. This in turn aids in the establishment of a poor self image, and our means of correcting this feeling is to invest in items that are supposed to make us feel better about ourselves as discussed earlier in the text. Look at how much we spend on clothing, makeup, high-heeled shoes, and plastic surgery. But it doesn't end there. No, in our pursuit to look even better, we get humongous bank loans to finance even bigger homes and fancier cars. We work like dogs so that we can buy possessions that will make us feel better.

We begin to look at other people as objects to make us look and feel better, too. How many times have we heard someone say that their significant other completes them? How many people do we know that wear their significant others like a charm dangling from a bracelet? And how many times have we heard of the "trophy wife"? That is, a wife specifically selected to make the man look like, what else? A "winner."

So we do what we have to do and take the steps we have to take to ensure we have people in our lives that *compliment* us. In the dating world, we sometimes spend a lot of money on and a lot of time with an individual in this quest. The more time and money we spend, we often believe the more someone is going to like us; so we spend more time and more money.

At the conclusion of a bad date or the revelation that a relationship will not be established following a series of dates, we complain about how we wasted both. It is almost as if that individual was not worthy of our time or our money because they didn't see the future that we wanted. Such a feeling of regret can easily force us into a shell, promising ourselves that we'll never put so much into dating again.

We could have simply avoided this scenario if we realized and accepted that *Dating Is Not an Investment*! This is something Kenneth had to learn the hard way. Since he spent so much money on his series of dates with Andrea, he felt as if she owed him something. In his mind, spending money on these dates should have led to Andrea taking him into her bed. Some could call that prostitution, but let's digress.

The whole premise of this book is to maintain minimal expectations in dating. And, since this is true, expecting rewards for time and money spent simply doesn't fit this concept. If we can't afford to pay for dates just for the sake of having a good time, then maybe we shouldn't be going on dates. Slavery is over, and plantations are a thing of the past. So treating people as chattel and expecting a return for services rendered is an ideology that needs to be made "history" as well.

To The Point

- Money is worshiped in our society
- We tend to be more cautious with and protective of our money than we are with our time, when time is the only one of the two that we can't make up or get back
- We should do a better job of determining how we spend our time earning money
- Question if all you do to earn money is actually worth it
- We can sometimes treat each other like objects; extensions of things we use or buy to make us feel better about ourselves
- In dating, we sometimes spend a lot of money on this quest

- When the date doesn't turn out how we expected, we wrongly complain about having wasted time and money
- No one owes you anything just because you spent a small fortune on a date
- Don't expect a reward for the time or money spent on a date

A Better Move

Plan a date that maximizes enjoyment without spending a great deal of money. The more money you spend, the higher your companion's expectation will be for the next date. The most important thing is to have a good time...and a "good time" should not be regrettable!

Contemplative Corner

1. What expectations do you have as a result of spending money on a date?
2. How is "time" treated in relations to "money" in your life?
3. How were you made to feel after someone has spent money on you?
4. Is the way you earn money or the time you invest in making money worth what you have as a result?
5. If you could earn money in a more fulfilling manner, how would you do it?

Melvin & Simone

Melvin's energy waned as he drove through the potholed streets of Martial Circle. The rotting southwest neighborhood was no where to be without an escort at this time of the night, but the frantic tone in Simone's voice rung with an urgency reminiscent of the call she placed when her sister died the previous year.

Having lost the taste for Simone's flavor long ago, Melvin cringed at the thought of spending another lengthy night listening to her whine about her loneliness and her need for him to love her. Her dramatics could have landed her a daytime Emmy, if she had the face for television. Melvin always thought Simone's heart was in the right place, but her luck was on an extended vacation.

****

When they first met, their simple flirtations quickly spun out of control, and before Melvin knew it, Simone was calling him her boyfriend. He didn't feel the need to correct her because he knew Simone would see the reality of their relationship when he landed that new job in Necropolis and moved away. Although he interviewed well for the position, the firm went with someone else, and Melvin found himself stuck in an old job and a new relationship he didn't want.

Simone knew how to comfort *her* man, and she was there for him to lean on when he was down. She made love to him with the ferocity of a wild orangutan, helping to strip Melvin of his sense of rejection and ease the tension that he, unbeknownst to her, felt when she was around. In a world where it was harder to be alone than to be with someone who didn't care much for you, Simone claimed Melvin as her own and was willing to do all she could to maintain what little bit of attention he paid her.

From time to time, the stress of being in Simone's presence would get to Melvin and he was always ready to flee. But he too had no desire to be alone. He had convinced himself that he would only stay with Simone as long as he had to, which meant until he finally moved away or until he met someone to replace her.

But there really was no chance for anyone new to enter into Melvin's world, because Simone always figured out a way to manipulate Melvin into spending any free moment he had with her. He found it harder and harder to tell Simone *'no,'* and when he would finally work up the courage to do so, Simone would sense the impending separation and a new, insurmountable tragedy would *somehow* fall upon her. During the close calls when she couldn't stir up some self-imposed drama, she had no problem drawing him into her bed with seductive looks and false assurances that she'd change.

He fell for it every time.

****

After a long day of interviews and a wonderful lunch date with a young lady he met in an online chat room, Melvin would have preferred to be pulling into an open space in front of his own new condo instead of searching for one in front of Simone's dilapidated one. As it was, Melvin didn't trust leaving his new Mercedes in the slowly gentrifying neighborhood for any length of time and definitely not for the amount of hours he knew Simone would have his ear.

Breathing the corrupted air of wet garbage and old houses as he walked the two blocks to her condo, Melvin wondered if it would be the night he would finally find the courage to conclude the dead-end love affair with Simone. Lunch with Eva had awoken his sleeping mind and reminded him just how miserable he was around Simone. He felt defeated after realizing the temporary satisfaction he felt with her was neither temporary nor satisfying.

Melvin prepared for Simone's normal hysterics as he approached her door. The light in the doorway flickered as he motioned to lift the knocker (a bad omen if there ever was one), and he slammed the brass against brass to indicate his arrival. The resounding *'clang'* reverberated throughout the entire neighborhood. Then, the door swung open to a darkened room, lit by a single candle on the kitchen counter. Simone hid behind the door until Melvin was well into the foyer. When she revealed herself, he was only minimally surprised to find her face streaked with tears. He fought to hold back the sigh that was building in his chest and tried to guess what problem Simone would be cursed with that night.

His answer lied in the palm of her hand in the form of a pregnancy test.

Waiting Too Long

We all make mistakes. That's just a part of life. We get things wrong so that we can learn from them and eventually make them right. What's dangerous is when we find ourselves in a cycle of making the same mistake over and over again. How many times have you made a mistake and said "I've learned my lesson" only to turn around and make the same mistake again...and again...and...again? It is safe to say that you really haven't learned your lesson, or you didn't take the lesson seriously enough to make a change. It is important to understand that the result of such cyclic mistakes can be catastrophic, if you don't stop making them.

In this particular narrative, our protagonist, Melvin, was caught in what we like to call *The Lover's Loop* (or the *Skipping Record*). Imagine yourself in a movie theater. You've got a big tub of popcorn on your lap and a half-gallon jug of grape soda in the cup holder to your side. Then, the lights dim and the movie you've been waiting all week to see flashes onto the screen. It starts with a *bang* (literally someone gets shot during the opening credits), and then it steadily goes down hill from there.

After the first twenty minutes, you are already anticipating the last two minutes of this twisted, monotonous, poorly scripted and horribly edited flick. You figure you might as well ride it out until the end, since you did pay for your ticket and you still have to finish off all of that popcorn and soda.

As the movie builds to its climax, you fight the urge to nod off in your now empty trove of popcorn, but you decide to hang in there. The crescendo builds, the scene draws to a close, and then--it skips back to the middle of the movie! After investing so much wasted time into such a horrible flick, you decide to stick it out just to see how it ends. But as it nears its end, it happens again—a loop back to the middle. So, you decide to give it just one more try, and as the movie nears its end, we are back in the middle again. The question becomes how many times will this have to happen before you get up and bounce? There's obviously a problem, and you sitting there waiting for it to fix itself is not the solution. Who's to blame if you decide to sit there ten more times waiting for a different ending than the one you saw coming from the beginning (or in this case middle)? The answer is YOU!

This is how our cycles can end up; it sure did for Melvin. As you saw, he could have easily saved himself from his ultimate fate on a number of occasions, beginning with controlling how fast he let their shared flirtations turn into a relationship he didn't want in the first place. Many of us make this mistake of letting a sexual excursion force us into a relationship (see: Sex Doesn't Make a Relationship). We can avoid this by not being so quick to bed the people we date, especially if we know we don't have any desire to be with them beyond that simple, instinctive act.

Another problem many of us have is waiting for a row of dominos to fall so we don't have to be responsible for changing our circumstances. We hope the collapse of things will naturally push us in the direction we want to go without having to do any of the work or take any of the responsibility. It would have been prudent for Melvin to have defined the extent of his part in the romance to Simone so that there weren't any misunderstandings. He was hoping that he wouldn't have to take that action, figuring that moving across the country would have stretched the cord until it snapped. And when the job didn't come through, he allowed himself to be drawn into Simone's web instead of realizing that by relenting he was really getting himself deeper into the situation. Be observant and see your surroundings for what they really are; recognize the difference between a web and a bed.

The domino effect analogy also holds true for Melvin's attempt at waiting to find a romantic replacement before sending Simone on her way. But he shouldn't have waited for someone to come and save him; he should have saved himself! As humans, we often put ourselves in a position where we wait for something to happen before we do anything about it. But until you take the first step, nothing is going to change.

The bottom line is that we need to be much more honest with ourselves and with the people we are dating. We try to convince ourselves of things that aren't necessarily true, and then we try to convince others. We tell ourselves that we need that sixty inch television when we know we can't afford it and a twenty-seven inch will do just fine; we persuade ourselves that it is okay to finish off the last half-gallon of ice cream when we know we are overweight, pre-diabetic, and have no intentions of starting our new workout regiment in the New Year; and we assure ourselves that we are doing the right thing by staying a little longer with Simone because she is having a rough time right now, when in fact she will *always* go through rough times until she changes her outlook on life. But more importantly, we convince ourselves that things with

Simone will improve when we know we didn't—and don't—want to be with her anyway.

No one benefits from deception in the long run. But Simone wasn't an innocent bystander either. She was stuck in a cycle of her own; a different kind of *Lover's Loop*. She didn't know how to be alone in her misery, and instead of dealing with her problems, she used them as bait to keep Melvin in her life. He became her emotional crutch.

We all have things that we go through and we all need support from time to time but, like a narcotic, it is never healthy to become addicted to it. Simone was addicted to Melvin's attention (see: **Building a Stalker**) and felt like she needed it to survive. Whenever he began to pull away, she found another way to reel him back in, and thus the loop was formed.

These two loops then interloped and formed a chain--or more appropriately put, a set of "handcuffs." Their concurrent cycles spun out of control and would soon affect a third life. The baby growing inside of Simone had become an innocent victim of two people's inability to learn their lessons.

To The Point

- Recognize those cycles in your dating life where you keep making the same mistakes or finding yourself in the same situations, even when you know better
- You can only blame yourself for the cycles in which you seem trapped
- Get to understand the root causes that prevent you from breaking those cycles
- Think twice, thrice, and four times before having sex with someone whom you have no intention on developing more of a relationship

- Don't wait for a way out of a bad situation to occur; take control and make the way out before the circumstances become direr
- Don't be greedy! Give someone the courtesy of a proper dismissal instead of holding until someone new/better shows up
- If you have to sell yourself on the idea of being with someone (making constant justifications), you probably shouldn't be with them
- If you have to trap someone into being with you, you *definitely* shouldn't be with them!
- Be careful of allowing your out-of-control cycles entangling the lives of the innocent

A Better Move

If you find yourself involved with someone who is constantly besieged by tragedy, encourage them to seek professional help. More than likely, all you are doing is keeping them company in their misery.

Contemplative Corner

1. What cycles do you find exist in your dating life?
2. How do you think these cycles formed and why have you allowed them to persist?
3. What has been the result of a sexual relationship with someone you had no intentions on developing a relationship?
4. What reasons have you used to convince yourself to continue a romance when you should have ended it?
5. What methods have people used to keep you romantically attached to them?

Eric & Mia

With the weight and the heat of her body becoming too uncomfortable to bear, Eric carefully slipped from beneath Mia's slumbering grasp and let her head fall gently to the pillow. Looking at the luminescent hands on his wall clock, he waited a moment before moving again, being sure not to wake her. He was not in the mood for her questioning and complaining at two o'clock in the morning.

Eric was able to roll out without causing too much motion on the bed but paused before putting on his underwear and making his way to the kitchen. Once he hears Mia's breathing deepen, lending way to a minor snore, he knew he was safe to walk a bit more heavily across the squeaky wooden floorboards. He closed the door behind him and moved swiftly down the hall to the kitchen to hydrate his sexually dehydrated body.

In the kitchen, Eric pondered a question while he guzzled down the contents of a gallon jug of water: How the hell did Mia end up in his bed again? She never called to say that she was coming over, and he hadn't invited her. What if he had other plans for the night? What made her think that it okay to show up, unannounced, at his door?

****

When Eric and Mia began seeing each other four and a half months prior, their chemistry was strong and their vibe was abundant. They had either seen each other or spoken everyday since they met, and once sex was thrown into the pot, they truly became inseparable. If Eric wasn't spending the night at her house, then she was at his.

113

To the average observer, Eric and Mia looked like a deliriously happy couple. They were playful and affectionate with one another in public, they would attend formal affairs together, and they even became close to one another's families. But they weren't quite boyfriend and girlfriend. Eric had known since their introduction to one another that they would never get to that level, but figured Mia would be someone decent to hang with in the meantime.

For months Eric engaged in normal courting activities. He would call or send her emails daily, take her out dancing or to her favorite restaurant, and would even romance her regularly with moon lit dinners, candle lit baths, and sensual massages in front of his fireplace. Mia adored this about Eric. She had received everything she'd been hoping for since she played house with her dolls as a child, and she had sucked up Eric's energy and attention like an industrial vacuum cleaner.

But time had a way of changing things when, in the previous month, Eric started getting burned out from all of the action and interaction. Slowly he began to pull away from Mia physically and emotionally. Other things, like work and friends, began to fill his time. The monotony of life with Mia had settled in and Eric found himself growing more and more bored with each encounter.

Mia's behavior started to change as well when she felt the distance growing between them. When he didn't call her, she'd call him. If he didn't answer his phone, she'd drive by his apartment complex to see if his car was in the parking lot. Even though she'd seen his car there several times before, tonight was the first time she was bold enough to knock on his door.

The further Eric pulled away, the harder Mia tried to hold on; the more Mia impressed herself upon him, the greater the force with which he pushed her away. Neither could formulate a sound hypothesis of the other's quickly changing actions or behaviors. It was a tug-o-war that neither side would win.

****

Lying on his couch to watch some little late night television, Eric's heart jumped when he heard something stir down the hallway. He sat up and looked into the darkness, but there was nothing there. As he reached to pick up his bottle of beer from the floor, a pair of size six socked feet appeared inches away from his hand.

Motioning for him to lay back down, Mia snuggled up to Eric on the couch, and pinned him in its corner where he would remain until morning. He had again lost the battle but he was determined not to lose the war....

Building a Stalker

In the previous chapter we discussed what could happen if we wait too long to be upfront with our negative feelings for someone. Keeping our intentions from someone could easily turn out to have life altering and disastrous consequences. But things don't always have to reach those extremes for the situation to be stressful on both parties involved in the matter. The person on the receiving end of the bad vibes sometimes gets the hint and simply moves on. He or she may even test the other person by distancing themselves to get a sense of where their mind is so they can make an informed decision and move on. Yet for others, they may choose to simply wear the person down in an effort to figure out where things are going. This is when the "what are we doing?" question rears its head.

It is natural for us to want an answer to our questions, and if we don't think we will get the truth directly out of our mate's mouths, we'll let their actions speak for them. We may easily be satisfied with one of these situations playing themselves out because then we don't have to do the ugly job of cutting the person off. Our passive-aggressiveness has done all the work for us.

If a terminated association comes by one of these means, consider yourself fortunate, since some people aren't very observant of the *signs*. Instead of making it easier by letting you off the hook, they dig the hook in deeper, causing you excruciating pain. Many times this action happens on a subconscious level. When a person can't figure out what's going on or feel you are not being honest with them, they cling tighter out of fear of losing you, sometimes exuding stalker-like behavior.

When They Go Crazy

In time most of these unhealthy affiliations will come to an end, and when they do, what is it that we proclaim about that person we've finally ridded ourselves of?

"S/he was crazy!"

But every person can't be crazy. It is just easier to dismiss each as so; easier to pass the blame instead of accepting it. It is always them; never us. But remember, to someone else *you are* the crazy one. Love *is* a two-way street, as the song goes.

Before you proudly make these declarations about anyone, **slow down!** Simple algebra proves that there is *one common denominator* in each of these situations and it doesn't take a calculator to figure it out. Is it really the case that everyone we meet is crazy and we just didn't see it, or have we in some way contributed to their irrational behavior?

Following Eric and Mia's story, we see two things that played a role in Mia's conduct. First, we must blame society as a whole. Women are trained for motherhood and marriage from day one. The toy houses we build for them; the life-like dolls and miniature, working ovens we buy for them, are all part of their preparation for the "responsibilities" of adulthood. The message they receive throughout these early years is "you will be a mother and a wife."

116

Then, the message changes around a woman's pre-teens just as they are beginning to put the toys down and turn their attention to the opposite sex. The new message is "be independent." We start to stress a woman's need to plan for her future, a future different from their mother's or their grandmothers; a future where they won't only survive in society, but where they will have the ability to thrive without needing to depend on the support of a man. The pattern we lay out for them is: graduate from high school and go to college; graduate from college and go to post-graduate school; take your advanced degree and build a successful career; and only after you've achieved all of that should you consider establishing a family.

So, for a period of time, women set aside the lessons of childhood to achieve the dreams of a successful adult life. Unfortunately, the subconscious desire for mating continues to play a part in their youthful relationships, making these interactions even more complicated. But they maintain their focus, and just as they are attaining their goals, usually in their late twenties/early thirties, biology takes over. The body's craving to carry a child goes into overdrive, which is a common biological occurrence that can't be stifled.

Then there's the social pressure. Women see their friends getting married and starting families, their "clocks" are ticking, and the early training they've endured has been so deeply engrained, many women can't see beyond it. With so many conflicting feelings and messages, it is easy to see why so many women are on the borderline of madness. This is the state in which Eric found Mia, and his actions are what pushed her over the line.

Men are reared differently. The messages we receive are both conflicting and imbalanced. We don't play with dolls where we learn to become nurturing; we play with action figures that fight and destroy one another. The messages men receive from society are to be aggressive, be protectors, and be conquerors; to be ready to provide for and protect our families. However, most men haven't the slightest clue of how to be nurturing husbands and fathers. We simply aren't taught how to fulfill these expectations.

As we reach our teenage years and our sexual desires come to the forefront (also a common biological occurrence), we are told to control our actions, but that's never part of our actual training. Instead, we follow the lead of others who have given into those strong urges. The message that we receive from our peers and the media is that we should be having sex, often, and with as many women as possible.

Eventually *we* are taught something during this period of our lives, ironically by women. We are taught that we have to *work* hard in the pursuit of our sexual conquests. The message that young ladies receive comes into complete conflict with the message men are being given. This is when we develop our *game* in an attempt to counteract women's training.

This is primarily where our attention stays. Not to sound too Freudian, but for many men our pursuits are influenced by our sexual desires, and they are incorporated into our game. In other words, the message we begin to receive as we reach our early twenties is to work hard so that you won't have to *work* so hard. The advertising companies know this for a fact. As they say, "sex sells."

In a man's mid-to late-twenties the message finally changes. It is then that we are told that we must settle down and start our family, but this is at the peak of our *game's* development. We are finally in a position not to *work* so hard. The ensuing confusion accounts for the majority of the irrationality found in men's behavior during the dating and courtship phase.

A Stalker is Born

A major mistake we often make in dating and courtship is jumping into the relationship head first. We give too much too early. Instead of taking the opportunity to get to know one another, we will see something we like and throw everything into it, or at least give the appearance of giving our all.

118

This is a lot like taking someone out to the most expensive restaurant in town on the first date. We've built a false expectation that every where we eat will be on that level. So, we keep dining at four and five star establishments, watching our bank account dry up, and then try to scale back, expecting our date to understand. Unfortunately, that's not what happens because with our help, they've developed caviar tastes. A fish sandwich and French Fries for dinner will no longer be an acceptable alternative.

Eric showered Mia with all of the attention she ever wanted. Because he enjoyed spending time with her, he felt the need to show her a good time despite having no intentions to establish something more formal and solid with her. He did all the things a man would do if he had a genuine interest in a woman; all the signs a woman would look for when she wants to be courted. As we discussed in the chapter "No 2nd Date," there is nothing wrong with continuing to date someone when it is not leading to a relationship. The thing that is wrong is when both parties are not honest about the intended goal—if there is a goal at all.

What we fail to understand sometimes, and many times ignore for our own satisfaction, is that these actions can easily be misinterpreted. Doing these things may be a part of our regular repertoire (our *game*), and we may think nothing of it. But for someone who is starved for love and affection, these actions matter a great deal. Not only do they become comfortable with the attention, but they may become addicted to it.

People are not dimmer switches. We can't turn a knob and then expect them to just fade away. When we try to flip that switch, the person's behavior begins to change to counteract the changes in our actions. They begin to call more often; they show up at places we don't normally see them; they attempt to spend more time with us; they may even set up *stakeouts* in front of our homes or show up announced.

Yes, we see this behavior as being out of the ordinary and extreme, so we attach a label to it: *crazy*. That label is such a general term and used so liberally that it unfortunately doesn't quite explain the conduct accurately. Even a psychologist may have a hard time identifying the affliction with which their patient suffers, and once they do, the therapist takes a look at the root causes for the affliction or what might have set them off. They don't just slap a label on them and send them on their way.

In this case, Eric's initial sense of affection followed by the retreating of his attention may have pushed Mia over the line. But her rearing to be a wife and mother didn't help much either. The difference in our rearing, as men and women, sets the stage for there to be serious friction in the way that we establish relationships.

As parents, we have to do a better job of showing our children balance and teaching them not to give in to emotional or societal pressures. We must teach them that it is fine to want and share love, but not to crave it and allow it to control their actions and behaviors, and definitely not to abuse it.

As lovers, we need to be honest with the people we interact with and not give in to self-serving behaviors that could potentially hurt the other person. If we see this same thing happening over and over again, it is important that we recognize our part in making it that way.

You take them out of their box; you dust them off; you build them up; you tighten their nuts and bolts; you polish them to a dazzling shine; and then you step back to admire your work.

Congratulations! You've successfully built a brand new stalker!!!

To The Point

- Be careful of someone choosing to hold on tighter when you passive-aggressively try to create a bit of emotional/physical distance

- Recognize your contributions to someone else's seemingly "crazy" behavior; everyone isn't crazy; your self-serving behavior may play a role in setting them off
- Women tend to be taught how to nurture, while men tend to be taught how to conquer; this can cause a conflict in each gender's approach to building a relationship
- Women and men's sometimes confusing, irrational behavior in relationships are rooted in the mixed messages we receive during our emotional development into young adulthood
- Be careful how much you give to a new romance; falling fast has its place, but not with everyone
- Your actions can be misleading and mischaracterize your intentions
- People can grow "addicted" to your actions
- Don't expect people to fade away when you lose interest; if anything, expect them to intensify their pursuit
- Try to gauge someone's state of mind about relationships before beginning a romance

A Better Move

If you are willing to play with someone's affections, be prepared to accept the responsibility of the outcome. Be clear in your intentions to yourself, first. Then, proceed appropriately. You may get away with being reckless with someone's emotions from time to time. But eventually the consequences of your actions will appear in the form of someone who is not to be toyed with!

Contemplative Corner

1. What behaviors have you displayed early in a romance that betrayed your true intentions?
2. How has someone's actions mislead your feelings?
3. How have people responded when you reversed what once appeared to be an aggressive pursuit?
4. What sort of behaviors have you grown "addicted" to in romances?
5. What in your rearing do you believe contributed the most to your approach to relationship development?

Carmen & Steven

Carmen had been looking forward to her trip for almost a month, and the weather was perfect for a good weekend of skiing—and snuggling. Spending the better part of her past two weeks being a nervous wreck to her friends, Carmen's spirit was finally at rest. After stressing over whether or not Steven would cancel on her, she could finally breathe a sigh of relief when he showed up at her house with suitcase in hand. She looked over at Steven knocked out in the passenger seat of the truck she rented for the weekend climb through the mountains and smiled.

Arriving at the lodge well into the late-winter evening, it took Steven a few minutes to realize the car had stopped moving. As he remained in the warmth of the truck to try and gather his bearings, Carmen checked into the main lodge and got the key for their cabin. She returned to the truck with a grin so big and bright, she could have melted all of the snow covering the mountain. Instead, she only blinded Steven who had begun to question what he'd gotten himself into.

****

Steven had been feeling the heat from Carmen since their first impromptu date. Meeting at a dinner reception for the city's top black accountants, one of Carmen's co-workers invited Steven out for drinks afterwards. The mutual attraction was instant, but Steven sensed a level of desperation from Carmen that made him a bit uncomfortable. She kept her claws dug in him all night, never letting him out of her sight and never letting him say more than two sentences to anyone other than her.

Because Carmen soon seemed to be pursuing Steven with great vigor, he thought that it was only fair that he let her know he wasn't interested in pursuing a relationship at the time. She shocked him with the confession that she wasn't looking to rush things either; she simply enjoyed his company and wanted to see where things would go. In Steven's mind he figured they were on the same page, but Carmen thought of it only as a challenge to change his mind.

Over time, Carmen would constantly call to ask Steven out for dates, and he would occasionally agree. She always showed up wearing sexy outfits, smelling like sweet pears, and carrying gifts. She wore her big heart on the outside and Steven appreciated that, but he never reciprocated. That didn't matter to Carmen, as long as he spent a little time with her.

As the holidays approached, Carmen knew she was wearing him down, but she was getting impatient with his lack of aggressiveness. Even though they were spending more time together and frolicking in the bedroom more times than not, it was only when she called him. She needed something big to knock down his walls and guarantee that she wouldn't be spending neither the holidays nor the cold winter alone.

Thus, the ski trip!

****

Lying in bed until noon, Steven and Carmen finally got up to start their day. Carmen kept Steven company while he was in the shower and ran down the newly shortened list of activities for the afternoon—along with her feelings. She saw it as a perfect time to gauge where Steven's mind-set was since she was essentially holding him captive.

She started by telling him again how much she really appreciated him coming up to the mountains with her and how important it was to her that they had gotten away from the city for a few days. Steven remained silent, washing over parts of his body he already cleaned, and feared stepping out of the shower and into the world that Carmen was trying to pull him into.

Realizing that she really hadn't said anything to invoke an answer or reaction, Carmen changed her tactics. Because Christmas was nearing, she asked Steven about his holiday plans. He quickly answered that he was going to his parent's winter home in the Florida Keys, being sure to emphasize how much he was looking forward to getting them *alone* for the brief vacation. Feeling a little shut out but controlling her defensiveness, Carmen let him know how nice his plans sounded and that he should have a really good time.

Carmen left the bathroom to get dressed, but the conversation was far from over. She figured she'd wait until dinner and, after she'd gotten a few drinks in him, she'd be able to get him to tell her what she wanted to hear. She didn't spend all of her money on a getaway weekend jaunt to go home boyfriend-less.

Courting's One-way Street

We are not only a nation of mass consumers; we have the impudence to be impulse buyers, too. If we come across something that we really want, we claim it in our minds before we even get our hands on it. This is an everyday occurrence for many of us, when we think about what and how we buy: we weren't even hungry until we walked past that pizza shop, so we stop in for a slice; we know we don't need another pair of shoes, but the flashy ones in the window are so cute, we go in and buy them—in two colors; we don't think the television in the living room is big enough, and in comes the seventy-inch widescreen!

This need for instant gratification has led some people into stealing, murdering, and bankruptcy. Some would view items that can turn people into such monsters of consumption "evil trinkets." Others view the desire as evil. The fact is the item is just a product or stimuli, and our desires are natural emotions void of judgment. We can suppress our desires, but eradicating them entirely is nearly impossible.

The biggest culprit is our lack of control over our actions. Our response to the stimuli triggers our desires and we allow our desires to drive our deeds. This seemingly weak human characteristic is actually a part of our system of survival. Our desires are motivating factors used to keep our bodies fed, to keep our persons safe, and to bond and procreate.

As society has advanced technologically, we have found easier ways to meet these basic needs. With our society's "get it now" ideology driving our desires, it is no longer about meeting our basic needs but a question of how much we will indulge them. As a result, people have found ways to exploit our ability to overindulge, and we carry that craving into every aspect of our lives.

Religion and law are two of the methods man has used to gain control our overindulgences. These two forces have established a solid fear by reinforcing the consequences of our actions; actions that are controlled by our desires. The partial failure of these two systems has been in cutting off the head (condemning our desires and penalizing our actions) but not instructing us on how to control our actions and desires in the first place. It appears easier to judge man's basic desire as being sinful or evil than to teach self-control, but in a world where the stimuli is so great and the fear of immediate reprisals are so small, the only thing we have left is our individual control over our actions.

You are The One That I Want

The way men and women interact with one another in our culture has more to do with filling our overindulgent desires rather than satisfying our basic needs. We are all walking-talking products, and marketed as such, becoming nothing more than stimuli to gratify each other's cravings. When we desire someone, we do all we can to make them ours (see: **Investments**).

For Carmen, Steven was such a product. She was very upfront about her desire for him and she immediately went into action to make Steven hers and hers alone. Steven was brave enough to let Carmen know that he wasn't interested in being in a relationship, which many of us don't always have the heart to do especially when we are still trying to fulfill some of our own questionable desires (see: **Building A Stalker**). Steven's behavior did nothing to quell Carmen's desires, and she remained convinced that she would successful court him and make him her man.

If we listen to any popular music station for a three-hour block of time, it will become overly apparent that Carmen isn't alone in her desires. Every other song is a confessional, exposing the artist's desire for a particular person. But that's the difference between art and life. When this type of pursuit is put on wax, not only does it come across romantic, but it sells records; when this display of admiration and wanting plays out in real life, it comes across more as begging and stalking. Not good.

Control Factors

What we've come to find in our many interactions between men and women is that there are established *control factors* for each. In biology, Natural Control Factors are defined as systems that limit the increase in the numbers of an organism in an ecosystem. This was instituted by nature as a check and balance system to keep one particular organism from becoming a pest. From a sociological standpoint, we can look at relationship control factors the same way. These are systems of control over the number of people and the fashion in which we allow them to enter our lives.

Women and men in our culture maintain one major control factor each: a woman's control factor is when two people will establish sexual relations; a man's control factor is when two people will establish a relationship. This isn't to say that the other's level of desire doesn't play a role in the establishment of either's control factor, but one has more say into when this activity will take place.

If we observe any of the youthful interactions between teenage boys and teenage girls, we will witness a woman's control factor being put into practice early in the dating process (see: **Building a Stalker**). As young men, women put us in a position where we have to beg, plead, and give up our control factor to get her to drop hers (literally and figuratively). A woman never loses her control factor; she will always be able to dictate when she will allow a *wanting* and waiting man to make love to her.

Somewhere along the way, the roles change. Men will dangle their control factor in front of a woman to encourage or even manipulate her into sex because at some point women begin to think they won't be able to coax a man into a relationship unless sex is involved. So she drops her control factor hoping that he will let his go, too.

Where this gets muddy is determining a man's willingness to give up that control factor; when a man is ready to be in a relationship. Generally, women are ready to establish this sort of association at a younger age and with less dating/sexual experience than men. Timing is everything (see: **The Interesting Chick**). If a man isn't ready to be in a relationship, then he just isn't ready. Coaxing, tricking, or convincing will only lead to an unstable courtship; it can even lead to an unstable marriage.

Think about it this way: if a woman is forced to give up her control factor, meaning a man forces her to participate in intercourse against her will, by all legal definitions it is considered *rape*. Let's ask ourselves, can a healthy relationship be established after one of the participants rapes the other?

This holds true for men being forced to give up their control factor, as well. If he is forced to participate in a relationship that he either doesn't want to be in or he just isn't ready for, it

128

is like raping him of his control factor or his right to dictate when such a bond can be established. Without question, the emotional and physical damage is nowhere near as severe, but the results of finding stability in a future union are the same.

Patience and Acceptance

The modern woman has a very hard time accepting this theory (as judged by her behavior), just as men in certain societies believe that a woman has no right to refuse him sex. The modern woman has learned to be in total control of her destiny (see: **Building a Stalker**), and the thought that they can't control this situation is almost unbearable. They believe that courting is a two-way street, and that they have the right to court a man. True, the right is there for them to do so, but the consequence for indulging such a desire will most likely result in an alienated man or a relationship in severely poor health.

When a man is ready to be in a relationship, he is *ready* (see: **The Interesting Chick**). If he is interested in pursuing a relationship, he will court you. You won't have to do any of the work, if you are a *willing* participant. Otherwise, a woman is robbing a man of being…a *Man*!

As frustrating as this may be, women will have to learn great patience if they desire a healthy relationship and eventually a fruitful marriage. Regardless of the cultural advances of the past century, there are still a few defined gender roles that should not be breached, no matter how blurry the line has become. This isn't to say that a woman must contain all expressions of affection. There is absolutely nothing wrong with letting a man know what's on her mind. The problem lies in her expecting a relationship to form when and how she wants it to because that's what *she* wants.

There's a big difference in hearing:

-"I like spending time with you!"

And hearing:

-"I want to be your boyfriend!"

A woman must learn to listen to what a man says, and not mince his words or turn them into what she wants to hear to be satisfied. If so, the only thing that will be satisfied are her ears, while her heart is left discontented.

The bottom line is man needs his time to mature and prepare for the responsibilities of being in a solid relationship. In the meantime, women may want to regain control over their own control factor. No matter how good you think you are (or how good you think *she* is) in bed, you will not be able to make a man stick around if that's not what he has in mind. It may work for a while, but the forecast for anything worthwhile and fulfilling is a stormy one.

To The Point

- Society exploits our basic needs and turns our natural desires into dangerous cravings and indulgences
- Social and governmental institutions deem our desires as evil and wrong, while supporting the structures that supply our indulgences; the same institutions fail to provide proper lessons on self-control
- Romantic interactions tend to reflect our sense of overindulgence more than satisfying our basic needs
- Relationship control factors have been instituted by society to establish a check and balance system between men and women
- There are two major control factors, one each for a man and a woman: women determine when sex will happen; men decide how a relationship will happen
- An attempt to gain control of the other's control factor can have a disastrous effect on the course of the relationship

- Part of the game men and women play is to use their control factor to manipulate the other to abandon their own control factor
- When it comes to judging a man's readiness to be in a relationship, timing is everything
- Men tend to be emotionally ready for a relationship at a more advanced age than women
- Although an extreme comparison, a woman may want to look at forcing a man, pre-maturely, into a relationship as emotional rape
- When a man is ready to be in a relationship, he is truly ready and there will be no reason for a woman to pursue him
- Women should be more patient and allow men to court them
- If you find yourself in pursuit of not just a man's attention and affection, but his commitment as well, he probably isn't ready to be in a relationship
- Be careful of interpreting someone's words or actions to fit your own expectations and desires

A Better Move

Women, make yourself available to a man's advances. That's not to say that you should leave yourself open to do all that the man asks or wait until that particular man is ready. But you should be ready to decide if you will proceed when approached. Men, you aggressively pursue other passions in your life. Why are you waiting for a woman to pursue you? If you want to share a relationship with her, let her know!

Contemplative Corner

1. In what ways has our culture, do you believe, influenced your cravings and desires involved in particular areas of relationship building?
2. Where has your sense of overindulgence led you into bittersweet romantic situations?
3. How have you used your own control factors to get a partner to do what you wanted?
4. How has someone demonstrated conflicting messages in their desire to be in a relationship?
5. What other control factors do men and women have when used by the other can muddy the establishment of a healthy relationship?

Allen & Robyn

On her way back from turning on the air conditioner in the living room, Robyn grabbed two towels from the linen closet and used one to wipe herself dry of the sweat running down her body. She couldn't believe how weary her legs felt beneath her. The heavy pounding of her heart forced Robyn to lean on the bedroom doorframe to catch her breath.

Allen looked on with pride from the far side of the bed. His smile sparkled beneath the beaming moonlight as his damped chest heaved up and down. He too was having a hard time finding his wind.

Still wobbly, Robyn made it back to the bed and passed the second towel to her magnificent lover. They looked knowingly at each other with matching grins and soak in the cool air blowing from the vent on the wall. As their body temperatures returned to normal, Allen slipped his arm beneath Robyn's neck and she rested her head on his chest.

Having run out of things to talk about months ago, they lied silently in their positions until the sun peeked through Robyn's bedroom window hours later. After one more quickie, and Allen dashed out of Robyn's door to beat the rush hour traffic on his way back across town.

****

As Allen drove home from his brother's house on a Friday night, a familiar, melodic ring chimed from his cell phone. Becoming giddy at the inebriated, yet seductive voice of the caller on the other end, Allen dug deep into his reserves to find the energy he needed for another romp with Robyn. It had been four days since their last rendezvous and four days since their last conversation. Their dialogue was brief and only consisted of four lines:

- "Where are you?"
- "Driving home."
- "I'm leaving the bar now."
- "Okay."

And so, the plan was in motion.

After an evening out with her friends, and reeking of alcohol and cigarette smoke, Robyn walked up to Allen's door. Without so much as a kiss, she walked directly to the bathroom where a towel and a t-shirt were ready and waiting for her. She took a quick shower and brushed the grimy taste from her mouth.

Turning off the bathroom light made the entire apartment pitch black, but Robyn knew its layout like the widow's peak in her hairline. She made her way to Allen's bed, Robyn felt around the cool sheets for the warmth of his naked body. Following a sequence of passionate kisses, it wasn't long before Allen's neighbors were once again woken by the sound of his headboard banging against the wall.

****

Ritualistically, Robyn's phone rang just after dusk the following evening. It turned out Allen's Saturday night plans had fallen through and he asked Robyn if she wanted to get something to eat. Lying lazily on her couch, Robyn had no desire to go anywhere, and suggested Allen pick something up and come over instead.

Forty minutes later, the couple sat on separate chairs in Robyn's living room, sharing a bucket of chicken. Eating take-out at one another's homes was nothing new. Despite seeing each other at least once a week for the past seven months, Robyn and Allen hadn't been out in public together since their second date. Instead, they found simple satisfaction lying in each other's arms and watching movies as a warm up to another night of marathon sex.

Such was the case that night as well. After their food had settled and the movie credits rolled, Robyn separated herself from the comfort of Allen's arms, stretched, and made her way to the bedroom. Allen wasn't far behind, stretching and loosening his belt buckle for what else? The same ol', same ol'!

G.D. & G.P.

In a world where epidemics of disease run rampant and unchecked by medical science; where the paternity of a child cannot be determined thus destabilizing the balance of a community (are you marrying a sister or a cousin?) and unnecessarily dividing the estates of wealthy men; where population control is necessary for a culture or society to sustain itself; where women die frequently during childbirth thus limiting the number of people to go around; and where personal responsibility cannot be enforced and women being raped is an everyday occurrence, let's face it: Sex *can* be a bad thing.

Historically, sex has been a troublesome matter for many societies, particularly the warring kind where invaders bore no responsibility for their victims. It is hard enough trying to control a conquered land, but if all of your soldiers are participating in raping and pillaging, you will have anarchy on your hands, and your claims at righteousness and enlightenment will have no merit. Edicts had to be erected to regulate some of these factors within a community or kingdom so that the rights of individuals were maintained, as well as the standard of living. Sex was by no means free; it came with a very high price.

There have been many societies such as this that have existed over time and some that still do. But in a place where laws are enforceable and serve as deterrents to poor sexual conduct, where many diseases are either curable or controllable, where birth control is readily available, and where paternity is easily discernable because of advances in medical science, sex is only a bad thing in the absence of education.

The days of casual sex being viewed as an unnecessary and evil indulgence are over. There's nothing wrong with the act of sex when it is performed with responsibility, understanding, and honesty. Throughout time, there have been many societies that have embraced this ideology and recognized the need to educate its citizens so that there wasn't any need to establish edicts. Sexual promiscuity can't be shoed away like a flying insect, but the education behind it can to be better promoted.

That Temporary Love Thang

There's a particular interaction between men and women that doesn't fit neatly into neither the dating nor the courtship category. There has been a song, a dance, and a movie named after this interaction. It is the Booty Call (aka Booti Call). But like with all things urban, when that term became passé, it evolved into "Friends with Benefits." For those of us who find ourselves in this sticky middle ground, we often do so while obeying certain unspoken rules. The following are a few of those basic (but silently understood) tenets.

We Are Not A Couple

The foundation of such an association is cemented in the understanding that you and the person are by no means a couple. There is no title of boyfriend and girlfriend. In fact, there isn't even courting. Simply explained, it is a mutually-accepted sexual alliance. Neither participant is there to fill the other's emotional need, only the physical. For this reason, the worth of a *booty call* is measured by the amount of satisfaction you derive from it.

Unless we are really, really desperate, we won't usually settle for something we can probably perform better on our own. But what usually leads to this sort of relationship is called *the GD* or *the GP* factor. We may have discovered that we share nothing in common with the other person, or there's something about them we can't get past that won't lead us to pursing anything more. The only thing that keeps us involved and engaged is the incredible sexual chemistry we share...*GD* or *GP*. As you've probably figured out, the "G" stands for *good* and the "D/P" explicitly stands for terms used to describe the male and female genitalia, respectively.

There is no disputing the shallowness of such an agreed upon union, and it leaves the door open for many misinterpretations and emotional misgivings. Still, many people use such opportunities as a means for transitioning out of a failed relationship without the emotional pitfalls of a rebound; as fill-ins until they meet someone with whom they can establish a serious commitment; or as a method to enjoy themselves as they pass time. We are not always in an emotional, psychological, or financial (relationships can be very expensive) position to be in a serious relationship, and we may have no taste for the in and outs of dating, but we still have a desire for the intimate touch of another human being.

However, problems can arise quickly within the *booty call* union. Undoubtedly, one or both parties will eventually "catch feelings." This is a natural outgrowth of spending time together, especially in such an intimate way, and it is for this reason that *booty calls*, by nature, are meant to be temporary.

We also may have to lie to ourselves about the reality of the situation to find peace within ourselves. The reality may be that we are not the only booty call on the other person's list (see: **Your Date's Date**). Even though the expectations in this union are low, we are still selfish and our egos traditionally can't handle competition in our intimate dealings. So, we contend with this from the standpoint that we are the only people on the list, and if we can't convince ourselves of that, we believe that we are the number one person on that list. It can be crushing to an ego to learn we aren't even in the top five.

Don't Ask Any Questions You Don't Want To Know the Honest Answer To

Although we were taught there's no such thing as a "dumb question," there is such a thing as too many questions. The danger of a *booty call* relationship arises when it is treated as an actual relationship. One of the special benefits of being in a committed relationship is getting to know all there is to know about your significant other. You are privy to info about their past, their future plans, how they are doing, what their day was like, where they've been, what they've been up to, etc. Sharing and having such info shared with you is a sign of trust, caring, and commitment.

In a *booty call* relationship, none of these questions are asked or of concern. In fact, the only question that is—and should be asked—is, "When are you coming over?" Sure, we wonder how the person's day is going just as much as we wonder about anyone else's, but we must be careful not to let that care interfere with having our desires met, if that is the kind of relationship you have signed up for.

We run into trouble when we begin to ask questions that don't concern us. Because we've been lying to ourselves in order to deal with the situation, we don't want to know that our sexual partner has been out and about, or has plans with someone else; and we really don't need to hear about their other, more recent, sexual exploits.

If we've asked that only acceptable *booty call* question and the answer we receive is not one we expect or want to hear, it is best not to follow it up with another. We must accept the answer and either make a *booty call* to someone else, or do something else with our time. When we forget our place in this other person's life and begin to ask questions such as,

"Why can't I see you?" or "Why aren't you coming over?" or "What are you doing?" we'd better be prepared to hear an answer that may not suit our fancy.

Lastly, as with any other sexual relationship, we do need to be safe. We will want to know the STD/HIV status of our partner and because of the limited questions we can ask about his or her life, we need to be sure that we are using protection each and every time we engage in sexual intercourse with them. Anything less—and especially in such a "laissez faire" sexual relationship—is downright stupid *and* deadly.

Our Time is Our Time (and No One Else's)
Just like it is in normal dating situations, one should always assume that they are not the only person on the *booty call* call sheet. Be realistic. Unless otherwise stated, there is a good chance that if we are engaging in this sort of relationship with a person, then they are possibly doing the same thing with someone else (see: **Your Date's Date**).

Remember, the only reason why we are participating in this type of relationship is for its physical benefits. This is why we don't ask questions that could lead to a truth we don't want to know. So, if we aren't enjoying the interaction, then there's really no need for the association at all, and it is time to leave the *booty call* behind.

Always Call Before You Come Over
An important aspect of *booty call* etiquette is to respect the person's space and privacy. This is not a stalking situation; there's no need to mark territory; there's no rummaging through each other's personal effects; there's no going where we are not invited; and there's definitely no showing up unannounced at the person's residence or job.

The suffix of the title is "call." It is basic *booty call* protocol that a call be made for any interactions to take place. It could be a call placed to schedule something a week in advance or for an instant connection (e.g., a "I'm just in the neighborhood" call). Regardless of the specifics, remember the key word is "call."

Sleeping Over Is A Possibility, But Not A Guarantee
If the *booty call* experience is truly enjoyable, then it is only natural you'll be exhausted and drift off to sleep. That is actually quite a compliment to our partner. After all, there's nothing like a good nap after such a passionate and enthralling workout. But don't get too comfortable....

Even though you may have just shared an explosive moment with someone, it is pertinent to remember it is still not a relationship in the traditional sense, and certain benefits don't exist. This includes going out for nights on the town, spending time with each other's friends and family, and most of all, spending entire nights or weekends together.

Yes, it can seem a little unreasonable to expect someone to finish pleasuring us, hop up, and hit the bricks, but in the realm of this kind of union, that's pretty much how it should go. But this agreement is something both parties may need to discuss. As the host(ess), we may not want the person's hot, sweaty body taking up extra room beneath our sheets until they are ready to leave. On the flip side, as the guest, we may actually prefer to sleep in our own beds for whatever reason.

There should be no expectation on either side that our *booty call* will include a "sleepover." We should feel free to ask, but if the answer is 'no,' there should be no hard feelings.

Conversation Is Optional, But Not Necessary
A common component in *booty call* associations is the lack of fulfilling, in-depth conversations. Because the affiliation is temporary, there really is no need to get to know one another outside of what has been established. The deep, intimate thoughts of the other person should not concern us, and we shouldn't be hurt if they aren't interested in our deep, intimate thoughts either.

140

However, all situations are different. You may be in a booty call relationship where both parties involved appreciate good conversation. Talking may be an integral part of receiving pleasure from the experience. Talking may be that foreplay that leads you to the boudoir. The important part is that both parties must agree. If your partner isn't in the mood for your yapping, respect the union for what it is, and keep your mouth closed.

This Affair May End At Anytime
Once again, a *booty call* by nature is a temporary, unspoken agreement. This means that you are under no contractual or moral obligation to continue the affiliation beyond the last time you participated in the act. There's no two-week notice and there definitely doesn't need to be a meeting of the minds. As a matter of fact, a "No More *Booty Call*" call doesn't even have to be made. When the relationship has come to an end, the matter is closed. Why you ask? Because there may be an endless number of factors and reasons that have lead to the end of this arrangement. Here are a few of them:

◊ We've out grown one another
◊ We've met someone else
◊ Our significant other was just released from jail
◊ The thrill is gone
◊ Someone has "caught feelings"
◊ We want more out of our sexual relationships
◊ Someone keeps breaking these rules!

Whatever the case, no one involved should be mad that it has come to an end. It may not have happened on our terms, but it was bound to happen eventually. Yes, we may want to continue, but if the person wants out, all we can do is wish them well and allow them to go on their way.

Don't worry. There's always someone available for a *booty call*—and you might not even have to pay!

To The Point

- "Booty Calls" and "Friends with Benefits" maintain a prominent place in our dating culture, and although seeming to exist without rules, these practices are governed by unspoken tenants
- These practices are seen as mutually accepted sexual alliances, absent the title of boyfriend or girlfriend
- The worth of a booty call is measured only by the amount of physical satisfaction derived, not emotional satisfaction
- Even though these practices can be filled with misinterpretations, people use them for such things as relationship transitions, romantic place holders, and sport
- Although some may resist it, booty calls will often evolve into something more for one or both parties involved
- For that reason, booty calls are meant to be temporary
- We often fool ourselves into believing that we are our booty call's only booty call, and if not the only, then the best booty call
- Booty calls are often void of questions that denote actual caring beyond, "when's the next session?"
- When asking questions beyond the basic one, be prepared to hear either an answer you don't want to hear or a lie
- The only other appropriate question should be addressed from the outset of a booty call engagement and has to do with the partner-to-be's HIV/STD status
- Because of the laissez-faire nature of a booty call relationship, protection should be used through out the term of the affair
- Because the purpose of a booty call relationship is sexual fulfillment, if the interaction ceases to be fulfilling for either party, it's time to end the affair

- Booty calls are to be arranged in advance, and drop-bys are unacceptable
- Don't expect a booty call to include a sleep over
- Conversation is optional but not guaranteed
- Don't question the end of a booty call affair, just accept it!

A Better Move

There's a certain amount of emotional baggage you may take on in such a partnership. It is easy to say that there is no room for emotions in a booty call relationship. But these emotions often develop naturally, and this is the part people often express to despise the most about these partnerships. If you are not open to the possibility of hearing about your partner's everyday life…don't participate!

Contemplative Corner

1. What expectations have you maintained even in a romance as limited as a booty call or friends with benefits?
2. What different senses of fulfillment have been achieved during booty calls?
3. How have partners over-stepped the boundaries of past booty call protocol?
4. How would you go about trying to turn a booty call into a genuine relationship?
5. How have your past booty call arrangements come to an end?

Glenn & Tequila   Keith & Sophie

The headboard had ripped away from the bed frame, half of the mattress was on the floor, and the sheets were non-existent. Glenn couldn't have guessed Tequila would be so passionate and wild. She caused him to make sounds he had only heard on National Geographic specials.

As they lay exhausted on the carpet in the middle of the bedroom, they both looked like war-weary soldiers after a battle on a hot summer day. The sting of sweat soaked into their many love wounds: the long scratches, the carpet burns, the passion bites, and the welts on their bottoms from the spankings. Talking was not an option; their lips were too raw and tongues too tired to form comprehendible sentences.

****

Waking in the middle of the afternoon, Glenn called Tequila to make sure she was alive. Her delighted giggle fashioned her answer. The longing for her attention multiplied and Glenn asked if she wanted to catch a movie later that evening. Tequila's energy was much higher than Glenn's, whose words drug as he spoke. She told him in her ever-chipper tone that she had plans to meet her girls out for drinks after work and that they planned on clubbing the night away. When she told Glenn where they'd be, he invited himself along so he could see for himself if she really was the tamest woman in her crew, as she proclaimed.

****

It was Friday evening and the Legion's nightclub was the place to be. With music thumping through the house speakers, Tequila and her girls grooved on the dance floor to the sounds of Naughty By Nature and their classic hit "O.P.P." With their hands and drinks held high in the air, they gyrated their bodies to the booming base.

Unable to see Tequila through the crowd, Glenn took a seat at the bar and scanned the room like a satellite looking for a stolen nuclear warhead. A few minutes passed before he saw the yellow spotlight shine on Tequila's glistening forehead. As much as he wanted to let her know he was there, he elected to wait until she left the dance floor before making his presence known.

Then his radar zoned in on an *enemy missile*: a grungy dude, wearing a pink shirt and sunglasses, had slid between all of Tequila's friends and was grinding on Tequila's plump posterior. What didn't sit well with Glenn was that Tequila didn't seem to mind. With this, he pushed through the crowd to intercept. As soon as he was close enough to her, he reaches for Tequila's hand and pulled her over to him. He embraced her with a bear hug and stared the other guy down until he left.

Glenn remained on the floor with Tequila until her friends were ready to hit the bar for round two. Once at the bar, Glenn hovered around the group of women like a fly until one of Tequila's girls built up enough nerve to ask him who he was. Glenn introduced himself as Tequila's boyfriend.

It was definitely to Tequila's surprise. She didn't even know she had one!

****

Down the bar a bit, Tequila's good friend, Sophie, was engaged in a flourishing conversation with a young man by the name of Keith. Screaming at the top of their lungs so that they could hear one another, they eventually agreed to dance and continue their deep discussion over breakfast the next day.

****

Breakfast naturally evolved into a whole Saturday spent together. First, Sophie and Keith walked their meals off with a stroll through Roosevelt Park. The crisp air and the changing foliage created a scenic backdrop of a romance that could potentially blossom in the coming winter. To the children frolicking in the playground and their relaxed parents, Sophie and Keith looked more like a seasoned couple rather than two people who had just met the night before.

As the evening stars made a guest appearance on the darkening sky, the temperature began to drop and the couple found themselves a little underdressed. The chill of the budding night gave them a good excuse to snuggle up to one another and move the date back to Sophie's place to warm up.

Keith popped a movie into the DVD player as Sophie prepared two cups of hot chocolate. She brought them out on trays with two containers of take-out Chinese food and set them on the huge bamboo coffee table in the middle of her living room.

Sitting back to enjoy *Mo' Betta Blues* as well as their dinner, both Sophie and Keith decided to save their whipped cream topped hot cocoa for desert. Even though the whipped topping had melted a great deal, it still left a creamy mustache around their lips after they took their first sips. The sight made them laugh, and they both gladly offered to help the other remove the sweet, sticky substance.

What started as a thinly veiled "good deed," ended in a long, sensuous kiss. Keith's hands excavated Sophie's body while she continued to explore his lips and tongue. After a short while, they realized Denzel, Joie, and Cynda were watching them as much as they are watching the movie, and they decided to turn off the television, leaving the room dark and filled with the sound of their moans.

****

After having spent the last twenty-four hours together, Sophie felt that it was time to start talking about their relationship and where they'd like to take it. Still lying within the warmth of her double-stuffed comforter, she wanted to know that Keith was going stop dating other women and be true to what they had together. There was dead silence. Worrying about what he might have gotten himself into, Keith looked out the window and wondered if he could make it back to his car without getting arrested for indecent exposure.

Sex Doesn't Make a Relationship

The only way to fully understand what truly pleases us sexually is to explore our sexuality. This includes both self-exploration and intercourse. Interestingly, we will probably conduct a lot more self-exploration in our lives, especially if we are not being fulfilled through intercourse. Without forming a healthy relationship with this side of ourselves, we are really missing out on something powerful. Talk to a divorcee who married their first sexual partner. After they've thrown themselves back in the dating world, they will proudly speak of having the opportunity to experience a new partner who actually had an idea of what they were doing beneath the sheets.

As a society, we have to let go of the shame and stigma associated with sex and recognize that, within safe practices, our sexual selves can be our most significant selves. In getting to know, appreciate, and love our sexual selves, the better aware we become of who we are, who we want to be, and who we have the possibility of becoming.

This isn't a decree to turn the world into a sex-crazed Babylon. We already live in an overtly sexual society, where our sensuous nature is regularly exploited for profit, and sex in all

147

of its forms is traded better than any hot new commodity on the stock exchange. Sex itself has become a commodity; more plentiful than platinum but just as precious (which definitely goes against the law of supply and demand). In what other corner of our culture can we find something so readily available and still retain so much value?

A major reason for this it seems, other than our nature to be sexual beings, is the negative stigma that is attached to sex. It is as if we are children and our parents are telling us 'no' in regards to touching a particular object. Because their explanation for keeping this object from us seems irrational in our minds, our curiosity and fascination for it grows. Our parents place the object on the coffee table where we can reach it but continue to tell us not to touch it.

But our parents can't entice us in such a way and expect us not to reach for the object when they aren't looking! We will jostle it about, toss it in the air, and spin it on its top, until it breaks or until we become hurt by it. Face it. It is our nature to be curious.

It is commonly known that we have a much more serious problem in the United States with alcoholism (where we are not suppose to drink until we are twenty-one years of age) than in some European societies where its citizens are allowed to drink as children. The more someone tries to keep something from us while flashing it in our faces, the more we desire that particular thing.

In relation to our sexual selves, these are our bodies and just as we need to mature mentally and become better in touch with our inner selves, our sexual selves need to grow and mature as well. This can aid in the development of us being better lovers, becoming more satisfied participants, and less obsessed with sex itself. Ultimately, it is about achieving balance between our natural desire and our actions.

The Body; the Prop

As a society, we often look for new ways to achieve old goals. When searching for a new job, it used to be as easy as being born into a particular trade. As men, we did as our fathers did. If our father was a blacksmith, we learned the trade from him and spent our living days as blacksmiths, too. Those were much simpler times.

Even though nepotism is still a frequently used technique in gaining employment, we utilize many different strategies in finding a job today. We work through recruiters; we take referrals; we post our résumés, search, and apply online; we take chances with blind walk-ins; and if we are lucky, we know someone who already works there that can get us in.

When it comes to establishing relationships, we employ many of the same techniques. Once again, in simpler times, marriages were arranged between families. If a husband died, his unmarried brother would take the widow as his bride. This system was so unbelievably void of the complexities in dating and courtship that we suffer with today, it is amazing that we haven't thought to revisit it.

Oh yeah, that little thing that we learned about in social studies class called the *Declaration of Independence* grants us the "unalienable rights" to "life, liberty, and the pursuit of happiness." No one has the right to tell us who we can and cannot enjoy a relationship with or marry.

So, we get dating referrals from friends and relatives; we take part in games like speed dating; we search newspaper personal ads; we go on blind dates; and we post profiles online hoping that someone will like our "'résumé" enough to send us a note. Culturally, we have devised a number of different and clever ways to gain attention in order to find love, using our bodies as props in the process (see: **Hiding You**).

Once we capture the attention of an admirer, we will often do whatever we can to maintain that interest. It is then that we continue to use our bodies as a prop. For many of us, the moment we share our bodies with someone, a sense of ownership

149

overwhelms our sense of logic and reason. Something as simple as a kiss can be like passing us the keys to a car; to some, engaging in intercourse is like planting a flag on a deserted island.

Our dating path can change direction with one paddle; with one *stroke*. The expectations that didn't exist prior to our underwear disappearing somewhere behind the couch have sprung to life like our libidos, because to many people, sex isn't *just sex*...sex is a *promise*. It is a promise that we will not share ourselves with anyone else. It is a promise that we are willing to consider a relationship with the person. It is a promise that we are going to share our hearts with that one person. Unfortunately, there is no validity to that.

Those of us who are blindsided by such expectations don't consider the repercussions of our lustful actions in those tense, blissful moments before "splash down." We become so engrossed with the act of procreation (without actually planting the seed) that all of our rationality dissipates as well. Our temptation for sexual satisfaction overrides our concern of the co-participant's possible emotional response to such an engagement. It is this lack of sensitivity and inescapable ignorance that produced the anxiety experienced by Keith in our story.

But Keith's response to Sophie's seemingly unreasonable line of questioning was not without its merit. Falling back on our *Declaration of Independence* once again, no one has the right to infringe upon our right to life, liberty, and the pursuit of happiness. In other words, Keith was not obligated to be with Sophie if that's not what he wanted. That could interfere with his pursuit of happiness. Unless discussed beforehand, a sexual encounter doesn't establish legal grounds for a relationship. Keith was not bound by anything other than his personal morality or responsibility; he was not obliged to consider anything further with Sophie.

Whether this was the case in this scenario or not, some people will use their body as a prop to establish a relationship.

They will use their "trap" as, well, a *trap*! Because of their personal beliefs and the value they attach to sex, they expect others to respect and uphold their "declaration," too, when in fact that's not guaranteed.

As we have seen throughout this book, relationships are very complex and like any complicated structure, they are not easy to construct and even harder to sustain. If it were as simple as just sticking a pole in the ground, anyone could hammer a rod into the White House lawn and call it home. It is just as unreasonable to expect someone we barely know to change their entire lives and stop all that they were doing prior to meeting us just because sex was had.

Body as a Possession

In the same way sex doesn't establish a committed relationship, it also doesn't make someone our possession either. The scenario involving Tequila and Glenn was a perfect example of how someone can become possessive of the person with whom they share their body. In their minds, they hold the keys; we belong to them now and they can *steer* us as they see fit.

It is very important that we understand what we are truly getting ourselves into when we have sex with someone new. Besides the fear of STD's and pregnancy, we may be taking on a person's emotional and mental baggage as well. Tequila may have really enjoyed Glenn's company and may have even considered a relationship with him, but until a commitment is discussed, she is her own woman with rights to do as she pleases. Remember our definition of the term *"single."*

She had every right to enjoy a dance with someone else, especially considering she didn't know that Glenn was watching her. There should always be some level of respect involved when we are in the presence of someone that we are seeing or dating, but it is up to us to draw that line and make our partners aware where it begins and ends.

As a matter of fact, even if we are in a relationship, our bodies are still our own. No one can tell us what or what not to do with them. Ownership belongs to us as individuals (see: **Dating Is Not An Investment**). If there is ever a time when we are being made to feel like someone's property, it may be the ultimate "red flag" telling us it is time to exit the relationship.

At the same time, it is very important to understand and respect the value someone else places on sex. This is a key reason why we need to be patient and take our time before we land in someone's bed or take them into ours. Sophie was not wrong for feeling the way she did, but both she and Keith were wrong for not having taken the time to learn more about each other, particularly their views on sexual relations. The less you know about someone before you become sexually involved with them, the more you may regret later.

To The Point

- Safely explore your sexuality, and come to better know, love, and appreciate that side of your character, without shame
- Our sexual fascination often begins as a curiosity with the taboo
- Dating and courtship are very complex institutions within our cultural system, and we employ many techniques to achieve satisfaction within these institutions
- We will often use our bodies as props to gain and maintain the interest of an admirer
- Once physical affection, from hugging to intercourse, becomes involved in our dating and courting experiences, we will sometimes become possessive of the person with whom we are sharing these intimate moments

- To some, sex isn't just an act; it is a promise of something more meaningful, even if no such verbal promise has been made
- Unless otherwise noted, a sexual encounter doesn't establish exclusivity in a relationship
- We will many times overlook this expectation that may exist in the minds of other people in our pursuit of sexual gratification
- Thus, the body/prop can be a trap for someone who doesn't want anything more than sex
- It is unreasonable to expect someone to change their entire dating lives because of one or even several sexual encounters, just as it is unreasonable to believe that someone might not want more after that same sexual encounter
- Ownership of one's body belongs to the individual, and you should never allow yourself to be treated as a possession
- Respect the value someone else places on sex, and don't expect that level to rise or drop to meet your own

A Better Move

Wait just a little bit longer before becoming intimate with someone. It is important that you know more than the nickname of the person with whom you are about to share both your bed and body, so that you may regret a little less later. Again, let the possible consequences help determine your choices!

Contemplative Corner

1. What value do you place on sexual intercourse?

2. When sexually involved with someone, how do you express your expectations for what that involvement means?
3. How did you develop your sense of sexuality?
4. Why do we tend to change our expectations once we become physical with someone?
5. How would you balance someone else's value of sex with your own, if uneven, to maintain a relationship, sexual or otherwise?

Epilogue

A Love Hostage Rant...Volume 1

Look, dating isn't about establishing a relationship, nor is it about having sex! Yes, we are all dating for the wrong freakin' reasons. When we are out on dates, we expect some kind of result, whether it is sex or a relationship. We've abandoned the concept of having a good time simply for the purpose of *having a good time*. Thus, we've abandoned simplicity and joy for purpose and results.

We enter our dates like we are going on a journey: we carry a map (i.e. other relationship books), an agenda, and baggage into our new ventures. This book is meant to help you abandon these ideals. There's nothing wrong with having desires. The key is acting or not acting on these desires. This means that dating really becomes a practice in restraint, and not giving into the desires or expectations that you carry with you everywhere you go and into every situation you find yourself.

In writing this book, I am not attempting to be a dating messiah. It is not my intention to turn your world upside down, change your system of beliefs, and lead you down a particular path. **It's Just A Damn Date** was written with the sincere hope that it would encourage you to be reflective. The point is to help you be more realistic about the potential outcomes of a date, but also for you to gain a better understanding of your past and current relationships so that when the time and person is right, your union will be healthier, stronger, and more fulfilling.

There is nothing in this text that is a quick fix to all of your dating and courtship problems. Only through great patience, compassion, and understanding will we build the kind of unions that last. We spend so much time worrying about what someone looks like, what they have, what they can do for us, and how we can change them—once again, trying to fulfill our list of expectations—that we never take the time to inspect if there is any chemistry or not.

Chemistry is something that must be felt mutually. The relationship that will eventually develop should have a deeper, unexplainable meaning than just how well two people can get along. Without the so-called "*It*" factor, any union could be destined to fail.

It is through these great experiences when we've explored our deepest feelings that we begin to thrive in the jaded world of dating. In holding onto these feelings, we will be better judges of the circumstances we find ourselves in. We won't settle for the love of someone with whom we have limited chemistry; we will desire greater passion, greater affection, and greater understanding in our relationships. But this can only be achieved through our experiences: good, bad, and ugly.

Hopefully, through the various relationship scenarios throughout this book, you were able to see that not all relationships are meant to be saved. And those that come to a close should not be used as hurdles that get in the way of our ability to connect, experience, and build with others. Those that end should not be mourned; they should be celebrated for the lesson—and in every relationship good or bad, you should *always* find the lesson.

As we continue to date, court, interact, explore, tear down, build up, evaluate and assess our interactions with others in that pursuit of happiness, it is important to remember that finding happiness in love always begins with finding happiness in one's self first. Love of self *is* the zenith of love itself.

OTHER TITLES BY TARIIQ OMARI WALTON

Fiction

Broken: The Misfortunate Misadventures of Mister Roland Montgomery (*City Tales Series Book 1*) – Released 2004

Crystal's Tears (*City Tales Series Book 2*) – Released 2007

Mr. Bachelor: Broken II (*City Tales Series Book 3*) – Released 2009

All Titles Available At:
www.omaribooks.com

ABOUT THE AUTHOR

Tariiq Omari Walton is an educator, author, motivational speaker, and television/radio talk show host based in the Washington, DC metropolitan area. He is also the founder, President, and CEO of Infinite Possibilities Entertainment, LLC and its divisions, Pharaoh's Tomb Production and Omari Books.

And be sure to check out our websites:

www.tariiqomari.com

www.omaribooks.com

www.viewsandvibes.com